Southern Light:
Twelve Contemporary Southern Poets

Ray Zimmerman, Executive Editor
Bruce Majors, Editor
Ed Lindberg, Editor

Ford, Falcon & McNeil Publishers
Chattanooga

Library of Congress Cataloging in Publication Data
Zimmerman, Ray executive editor
Southern Light, Title

ISBN 978-0-9827252-2-1

Manufactured in the United States of America

First Edition

Graphic Artist - Rocio Almeida
Line Editor - Cathy Kodra

Advance Praise

These Southern Light voices cast a keenly perceptive and understanding, western, yet universal beam, penetrating its way upon a quiet, morning world, still asleep. From "Firecrackers at Christmas" to "Thanksgiving 1956," from "Cutting My name in a Tree" to "Planting Buckwheat," from "Just Another Mary Jane joke" to "Where Wedding Bands Go," from "What is Left in Old Houses" to "Daybreak at the Old City Park," from "Reincarnation" to "Discourse of Pleasure," these poems uncompromisingly push forth into illumination, lighting up the whole sky. And we, like birds, glide through pages of remembering, pages of forgetting and pages of not knowing, but understanding. Tossing and turning, transforming stress into moments of revelation, moments of redemption, moments of forgiveness, these writers respond to their own questioning. In this collection of landscapes and backdrops, witness and testimony celebrate the gods of all things small. Like an old '56 Ford pickup truck navigating and negotiating the ruts of a hard, Georgia, red clay, backwoods road, these writers know that headlights are not the only lights that get us through a Southern night. *-Earl S. Braggs, author of Walking Back from Woodstock, After Allyson*

Once every generation a collection of poetry comes along that captures the "gift of tongues" in the South. Southern Light is such a collection, at once, illuminating and wise, daring and ambitious. Recovering acclaimed out-of-print poems by Robert Morgan, one of the most beloved laureates in the region, among emerging and important voices, and edited by poets Ray Zimmerman, Ed Lindberg and Bruce Majors, Southern Light speaks out of the dark with a breathtaking range of voices, stories, even secrets. From the lives hidden behind the No Vacancy signs at neon landmarks, to the red spars of morning light that lean across the tops of trees, to daybreak at a city park, Southern Light transcends the borders of most regional collections, reminding readers of the joyous burdens of every day life. The nationally acclaimed poet Penny Dyer admonishes: "Look at your fingertips / or the plowed fields of your palms. / Everything man touches / the shined marble of museum floors, / rhombuses of wiped windows, / the swept sidewalk of your neighbor's home, / all of them, if you look close enough / are matched fingerprints." Southern Light is a timely and valuable collection of literary fingerprints and unmatched narratives for our times. *-Jeff Biggers, author of Reckoning at Eagle Creek, The United States of Appalachia*

Foreword

When Bruce Majors, Ed Lindberg and I sat out to assemble this anthology, we wanted to bring some emerging writers to the world's attention. A few well established poets joined our ranks, which gives the volume valued authority. As we added more poets to the collection, many of them suggested others we could include.

We stopped with the current contributors because we wished to provide depth of exposure for the writers involved. This is in marked contrast to a typical anthology which gives only a sampling of each author, with more breadth than depth.

I originally envisioned a collection of 140 poems, with twenty poems from each of seven authors. The number of contributors grew like kudzu, with a corresponding decrease in the number of poems from most.

Undoubtedly, we have left out several deserving poets from our region. This may be addressed by future anthologists, but for now I am pleased to present this collection of twelve regional authors. Each is worthy of reading and rereading. I hope you enjoy reading our Southern Light much more than we enjoyed assembling the collection.

Ray Zimmerman

Introduction

The poets in this volume have one thing in common. All are native to or have spent some sizeable portion of their lives in the distinct physical and cultural geography of the Southern United States. This book presents some of the best examples of poets currently working in the South. Some of these poets are well recognized while others are not widely known. Some are academicians; some shun the academy. Some are young; several are past sixty. In this volume we show the vigor and variety of contemporary Southern poets.

The label "Southern" can be expressed as a form of striking depiction supported by a certain perspective on the contents of the heart. A huge body of written work from poems to novels to songs continues to come from this geography. This intense flow of words may have some common source and influence. Some suggested origins of this diverse output of work have been religion, separatist politics, ethnicity, the language of the King James Bible, and Elizabethan English. Other components include land worked, struggled and fought for, the hard dignity of integrity, and various story telling forms and traditions.

I think whatever informs and impacts the lands of place and heart is the definition of what generates this considerable literary effort labeled "Southern". A central component of important stories is the cost of things and how things come to be. If they are anything, good poems are stories and are put down to tell of what has come upon or to their writer from whatever source named or unnamed, nameable or unnamable. Experience is the heat that ferments the passion to tell.

Ed Lindberg

Table of Contents

Robert Morgan

Robert Morgan is the author of eleven books of poetry, most recently *The Strange Attractor: New and Selected Poems* and *October Crossing*. He has also published eight volumes of fiction, including *Gap Creek* and *Brave Enemies: a Novel of the American Revolution*. Winner of the Hanes Poetry Award from the Fellowship of Southern Writers, the North Carolina Award, and the Appalachian Heritage Award, he has also received an Academy Award in Literature from the American Academy of Arts and Letters. *Gap Creek*, a *New York Times* bestseller, also received the Southern Book Award. A nonfiction book, *Boone: A Biography*, received the Kentucky Book Award in 2008. A native of western North Carolina and a member of the Fellowship of Southern Writers, he has taught since 1971 at Cornell University where he is now Kappa Alpha Professor of English.

Radio

In the corner farthest from the fire,
a safe of carved oak,
cabinet of voices.
The gothic windows stretched with cloth
hide a powerful hum when Grandpa
rolls the knob and the numbers
light up as the needle
passes in its window.
He hunts for the combination.
Birds back somewhere among
the preachers, static, whine
and whistle late at night from forests.
I want to reach in there
and find the jars that sing,
and watch through a gap in the back
the vials glowing in the much of wires,
a throbbing in the metal
where the languages of the air
are trapped and spoken.
That space unreachable in the small light,
poisoned by electricity.

The Gift of Tongues

The whole church got hot and vivid
with the rush of unhuman chatter
above the congregation,
and I saw my father looking at
the altar as though electrocuted.
It was a voice I'd never heard
but knew as from other centuries.
It was the voice of awful fire.
"What's he saying?" Ronald hissed
and jabbed my arm. "Probably Hebrew."
The preacher called out another
hymn, and the glissade came again,
high syllables not from my father's
lips but elsewhere, the flare of
higher language, sentences of light.
And we sang and sang again, but
no one rose as if from sleep to
be interpreter, explain the writing
on the air that still shone there like
blindness. None volunteered a gloss
or translation or receiver
of the message. My hands hurt
when pulled from the pew's varnish
they'd gripped and sweated so. Later,
standing under the high and plain-
sung pines on the mountain I clenched
my jaws like pliers, holding in
and savoring the gift of silence.

When He Spoke Out of the Dark

When he spoke out of the dark I
had not seen him sitting there in
a lawn chair on the grass resting
in his white painter's overalls
and gray sweatshirt and cap, gray hands,
easing after the long workday.
For the milking was over, and
weeds pulled for the hog, kindling had
been cut and the painting done,
the masonry and carpentry,
the holes had been dug, the corn hoed,
beans carried out of mud, the ditch
opened, the corn gathered and heaved
into the barn loft and shelled and
carried to mill. And there he sat,
tired, where I had not seen him,
looming to my dark-adjusting eyes
white and smokelike out of the depths
of night, and spoke close as anyone
in the after-supper darkness,
rest-happy from the long workday.

Robert Morgan

Uncle Robert

M Sgt. Robert G. Levi   1915-1943
Serial No. 34119284
813th Bomb Sqdn.
482nd Bombardment Group
Eighth Air Force

In the little opening in the woods
your cot springs were a crisp red wool
on the moss. While we raked leaves
for the cowstall Grandma told me how
you came up here on summer afternoons
to read and paint and sleep after
working the hootowl shift at the cottonmill.
You must have meant to return to leave
your couch on the innerspring moss
on the mountainside.

                 The metalwork you did
in the CCC – toolbox, a vase, buckets
thick as stoves – was scattered through house
and barn. I lost your flies and tackle
in the weeds above the garden, and stuck
your chevron patches to my flannel shirt.
In the messkit returned from England
I fried sand like snow, and found
the picture of your fiancée in the cedarchest.

It was hinted I was "marked" somehow,
not only by your name, but in some way
unexplained was actually you. Aunts and cousins
claimed we favored and I spoke with your stammer.
Your paintings watched me
from the bedroom wall and mantel

and your poem clipped from the paper
yellowed among the rationbooks. I inherited
your Testament with its boards of carved cedar,
and the box of arrowheads you picked
from the dust of bottomlands on Sunday afternoons
like seeds and teeth of giants.

No one opened the steel coffin sent back
to see what bone splinter or rags
had been found where the B-17 novaed
above East Anglia. I touched the ribbons
and medals in the bureau, the gold buttons.
Your canoe lay in the barnloft for years
between the cornpile and the wall, heavy
with dust as the boat in a pyramid
and tracked by mice and swallows. The paint
and canvas curled away from cedar slats.
I meant to use it someday but never dared:
it was not creekworthy without new skin
and too heavy for one to carry. I turned
it over and looked into the belly
and sat on the webbed seat, rocking
on the corn-bearinged floor. Once hornets
built in the prow what I imagined
was a skull with honey brains. On snowy days
I sat there and paddled across the wilderness
of loft dark. The summer before you left
you portaged to the river and back,
then carried the canoe up there.
Something was always scary about the craft:
each time I turned it over fearing to see
a body inside. It lay among the shucks
and fodder as though washed up by a flood
and stranded forever.

One day I found your bugle
in the attic, velveted with dust and lint.
The brass felt damp with corrosion,
the bell dented and dark as leather.
I took it out behind the house and,
facing west, blew into the cold mouthpiece
a hopeful syllable. The metal trembled
and blared like a sick steer, went quiet.
I poured all my body heat into the barrel
and a sour flatulence shook out and echoed
off the mountains. I made half-musical
squeaks and bursts till dizzy, aiming vowels
like watermelon seeds into the tube.
When the groans returned from Buzzard Rock
I thought they must be wails from the cove
for someone dead, and nothing I had sent,
or the ghost of a train lost in the valley
and relayed like an aural mirage from
the past still with us and talking back.

The flag that draped your casket was kept
folded in the trunk. They said
I had the high-arched "Levi foot"
like you, and your quick laugh. I was told
you made your own marbles as a boy
by rolling branch clay into balls and baking
in the oven. Mama liked to take out
of cloth a clay statue of a naked man
face down in the dirt which you once
modeled and called "The Dying Warrior."
I marveled at the cunning work of leg
and tiny arm and spilling hair, and touched
your fingerprints still clear on the base.

Passenger Pigeons

Remembering the descriptions by Wilson
and Bartram, and Audubon and other
early travelers to the interior, of the sky
clouded with the movements of winged pilgrims
wide as the Mississippi, wide as the Gulf
Stream, hundred-mile epics of equidistant wings
horizon to horizon, how their droppings
splashed the lakes and rivers, how
where they roosted whole forests broke down
worse than from ice storms, how the woods floor
was paved with their lime, how the settlers
got them with ax and gun and broom
for hogs, how when a hawk attacked
the endless stream bulged away
and kept the shift long after
the raptor was gone, and having read how
the skies of America became silent, the fletched
oceans forgotten, how can I replace
the hosts of the sky, the warm-blooded jetstreams?
To echo the birdstorms of those early
sunsets, what high river of electron, cell and star?

Sidney Lanier Dies at Tryon 1881

The chill mountain air grew stingy
with oxygen after the long
carriage ride from Fletcher across
the Ridge and down the Thermal Belt
to the house outside Tryon.
Two months of camping on the peaks
only made the world more hazy,
ghostlike, and the summit winds had
sucked away his breath, and stolen
his voice, the form and duration
of English phrasing he'd worked so
to make measurable, to set down.
And the current pouring from his lips
into the flute had vanished
and only turbulence and coughs
and random winds were left gusting,
subsiding in his head. The blood
seemed at times to want to break
out of his heart and through the skin
of his forehead to taste air, to
quench its awful heat. The blood he
spat and blood humming in his ears
and in the manly condition
only Mary understood made
him think of sunrise, the rose-lit
mornings in army camps, in
prison pits and mud. The one
oratorio, all notes and language,
seemed red as coals, red as his
syllables, while the night he'd married
hovered near, and his son the shadow,
and the world somewhere gaudy and
subtle as Shakespeare drew further

back, swam on the higher oceans.
The black peaks beyond the house looked
down, and there was a certain phrase,
a ripple, a little turn on
the flute he must try to recall,
that ran the same as the dark ridge
looming at the window yesterday,
and he could almost remember
the precise fingering, the pause
and the continuing line, just
as the world became visible.

Broomsedge

There is no whisper like the lisp
of broomsedge on the hill, the long
sigh of the afternoon feeling
around the pasture and combing
out the blondest grass, the wheaty
stalks with thistle in their ears
that lean and straighten away from
the prevailing voice. On the poor
land, the grave land, the oldest fields,
the broomsedge whisks and strokes bright
rumor from the air, a vowel,
a long slow ease of song below
the threshold of song, an ancient
lull almost unheard but coming
along the world's edge over
clay and subsoil, like the faint
music of ancestors in our
bloodsleep who tell with bending blade
and downy seed everything we
know and nothing we remember
at this poorest elevation.

Yellow

May is the yellow month. At this
latitude the woods are a fog of different
yellow-greens as first leaves
open pages and new twigs on the willows
grow bright as chicken fat.
In every yard the daffodils and dandelions,
and clouds of wild mustard light
the open fields, even as wind
bruises cowlicks in the rye. Along
highways and parks forsythia
sprays its heat, and fire rinses seedbeds
of old stalks at dark. The day begins
in a golden antiquity, flushing
the ridges so they echo inside the room
where flesh stretches into flower, where
even the interior of night is saffroned
the most erotic color of touch and know.

Manure Pile

Heaped gold and powerful behind the barn.
The crust, faded by weather, almost
never freezes, steaming off snow with the fever
of its inner work. Birds worry
the seeds exposed by rain.
Black chemistry of the core
nurses weeds on the baked hide
while the yard is frost-dead. Once
a little chick peeped from its straw
in January, hatched by the warmth.
The matter dug from its side for fields
is too strong even for worms to live in,
sealed years by the ammonia.
Haunted in the hot months by a genie
of flies, it jewels the downwind.
Sundays the many purple butterflies
that suck its inks shiver off into the sky
where carillons of convection ring.

Bellrope

The line through the hole in the dank
vestibule ceiling ended in
a powerful knot worn slick, swinging
in the breeze from those passing. Half
an hour before service Uncle
Allen pulled the call to worship,
hauling down the rope like the starting
cord of a motor, and the tower
answered and answered, fading
as the clapper lolled aside. I watched
him before Sunday school heave on
the line as on a wellrope. And
the wheel creaked up there as heavy
buckets emptied out their startle
and spread a cold splash to farthest
coves and hollows, then sucked the rope
back into the loft, leaving just
the knot within reach, trembling
with its high connections.

Elmer's Seat

Elmer sits for years on the bank
above the meadow, watching his
cow graze. There is a seat pressed in
the leaves that seems the bed of some
animal scooped out of the hill
and shaded by the margin oaks
and white pine grove. The nest is both
leaf-lined and needle-cushioned, new
with every wind. He grazes
his cow in the spring-glade and watches
her hour by hour and afternoon
by afternoon, not moving, still as
when he lay two days in Flanders
mud and bodies, playing his corpse
and watching the sky change sides. Ground
squirrels work around and rabbits
and woodpeckers gather and leave
while hepaticas shine and leaf
out into summer as he looks
and the Jersey changes spots and
trees color and airplanes get higher
above and quieter until
they are almost invisible
except for cobwebs floating down.

Sigodlin

When old carpenters would talk of buildings
out of plumb or out of square, they always
said they were sigodlin, as though anti-
sigodlin meant upright and square, at proper
angles as a structure should be, true to
spirit level, plumb line, erect and sure
from the very center of the earth, firm
and joined solid, orthogonal and right,
no sloping or queasy joints, no slouching
rafters or sills. Those men made as they were:
the heavy joists and studs yoked perfectly,
and showing the dimensions themselves, each
mated pair of timbers to embody
and enact the crossing of space in its
real extensions, the vertical to be
the virtual pith of gravity, horizontal
aligned with the surface of the planet at
its local tangent. And what they fitted
and nailed and mortised into place, downright
and upstanding, straight up and down and flat
as water, established the coordinates
forever of their place in creation's
fabric, in a word learned perhaps from
masons who heard it in masonic rites
drawn from ancient rosicrucians who
had the term from the Creek mysteries'
love of geometry's power to say,
while everything in the real may lean just
the slightest bit sigodlin or oblique,
the power whose center is everywhere.

Inertia

There is such a languor to matter,
every mass asserting presence
while soaring in its stasis.
Electrons spin and molecules
twitch, yet the material resists
all change of direction, defends
its momentum and moment, in
the reverie of substance, the
immobility and dream of
the body's authority of weight,
remaining undisturbed by poise
of precedence, occupation,
reluctant as a bear to wake
from the immanence and ponder,
the gravity of mere artlessness.

Radiation Pressure

Though in our slow world of friction
and gravity we hardly feel it,
light presses on the things it hits,
pouring on a stream of photons
against each surface, raining down
forever on each face and facet,
propelling bodies in deep space,
beyond significant gravity,
away from the white source. They flee
the emanation, as radiance
pushes down and washes all matter
in its way, sweeping dust and crystal,
even little moons and planets,
toward darkness, clearing way for
solar wind to thrill without
obstruction. Though here where sunlight
touches a hand or lip we feel
only slightest pressure, a kiss,
a breath come across the mighty
distances to urge away, while
we're stayed by our very sadness.

Spirit Level

Shifty-eyed as an auctioneer, the bubble
hides quick. Every touch makes it overshoot
its lines. The nervous little fish
of emptiness backs, then rushes forward
in the vein of elixir, hunting
high ground, hoping for the outlet
to burst into the open. No rest except
when aiming at the center of the sky
and at the center of the earth.
Put to sleep by accuracy.

Heaven

And yet I don't want not to believe in,
little as I can, the whoosh of souls
upward at the Rapture, when clay and ocean,
dust and pit, yield up their dead, when all

elements reassemble into the forms
of the living from the eight winds and flung
petals of the compass. And I won't assume,
much as I've known certain it all along,

that I'll never see Grandma again, nor
Uncle Vol with his fabulations,
nor see Uncle Robert plain with no scar
from earth and the bomber explosions.

I don't want to think how empty and cold
the sky is, how distant the family,
but of winged seeds blown from a milkweed field
in the opalescent smokes of early

winter ascending toward heaven's blue,
each self orchestrated in one aria
of river and light. And those behind the blue
are watching even now us on the long way.

Rearview Mirror

This little pool in the air is
not a spring but sink into which
trees and highway, bank and fields are
sipped away to minuteness. All
split on the present then merge in
stretched perspective, radiant in
reverse, the wide world guttering
back to one lit point, as our way
weeps away to the horizon
in this eye where the past flies ahead.

Audubon's Flute

Audubon in the summer woods
by the afternoon river sips
his flute, his fingers swimming on
the silver as silver notes pour

by the afternoon river, sips
and fills the mosquito-note air
with silver as silver notes pour
two hundred miles from any wall.

And fills the mosquito-note air
as deer and herons pause, listen,
two hundred miles from any wall,
and sunset plays the stops of river.

As deer and herons pause, listen,
the silver pipe sings on his tongue
and sunset plays the stops of river,
his breath modeling a melody

the silver pipe sings on his tongue,
coloring the trees and canebrakes,
his breath modeling a melody
over calamus and brush country,

coloring the trees and canebrakes
to the horizon and beyond,
over calamus and brush country
where the whitest moon is rising

to the horizon and beyond
his flute, his fingers swimming on
where the whitest moon is rising.

Robert Morgan

Firecrackers at Christmas

In the Southern mountains, our big
serenade was not the Fourth but
always Christmas Eve and Christmas.
Starting at midnight the valleys
and branch coves fairly shook with barks
of crackers, boom of shotguns, jolt
even of sticks of dynamite.
You would have thought a new hunting
season had begun in the big-star
night, or that a war had broken
out in the scattered hollows: all
the feuds and land disputes come to
a magnum finale. The sparks
everywhere of match and fuse
and burst were like giant lightning bugs.
Thunder doomed the ridges though
the sky shone clear and frost sugared
the meadows. Yankees were astonished
at the violence and racket
on the sacred day, they said, as
cherrybombs were hurled into yards
and placed expanding mailboxes
same as Halloween. Perhaps the custom
had its origins in peasant-pagan
times of honoring the solstice
around a burning tree, or in
the mystery centuries of
saluting the miraculous
with loudest brag and syllable.
Certainly the pioneer had
no more valuable gift to bring
than lead and powder to offer
in the hush of hills, the long rifles

23

their best tongues for saying the peace
they claimed to carry to the still
unchapeled wilderness, just as
cannon had been lit in the Old
World to announce the birth of kings.
They fired into the virgin skies
a ceremony we repeated
ignorantly. But what delight
I felt listening in the unheated
bedroom dark, not believing in
Santa Claus or expensive gifts,
to the terrible cracks along
the creek road and up on Olivet,
as though great rivers of ice were
breaking on the horizon and
trees were bursting at the heart
and new elements were being born
in whip-stings and distant booms
and the toy chatter of the littlest
powder grace notes. That was our
roughest and best caroling.

Lightning Bug

Carat of the first radiance,
you navigate like a creature
of the deep. I wish I could read
your morse across the night yard.
You body is a piece of star
but your head is obscure. What small
photography! What instrument
panel is on? You are winnowed
through the hanging gardens of night.
Your noctilucent syllables
sing in the millennium of
the southern night with star-talking
dew, like the thinker sending nous
into the outer stillness from
the edge of the orchard country.

Robert Morgan

Comments on Twenty Poems

These twenty poems are reprinted from three books long out of print, *At the Edge of the Orchard Country*, 1987, *Sigodlin*, 1990, and *Green River*, 1991. In the period when this work was written, I was concentrating on poetry in a more narrative and conversational voice than was evident in much of my earlier work. While some of these poems are in free verse, many are written in eight syllable lines. I was already being drawn toward an iambic or trochaic tetrameter line.

Though many of the poems are about the rural world of the Blue Ridge Mountains of North Carolina where I grew up in the 1940s and 1950s, some concern science, tools, and instruments. I have always been drawn to write about history, folklore, and the work we do in our daily lives. To a great extent, our work defines us. It is work that enables us to get on with our lives. A job well done gives us our greatest satisfaction, whether a plowed field or a poem.

It has been said that poetry is a way of barking at the moon. I suspect our ancestors developed language for the thrill of finding the right names for things and the pleasure of telling a story. We write poetry to remind us of what we have forgotten, to celebrate the cycles and passing of the seasons. We write to honor those who have gone before us. Poetry moves by repetition and progression. As alchemy has been called "the art of far and near," so poetry connects at once with both intimacy and the remoteness of a crystal or a star.

I write to celebrate memory, mountains, mystery, machines and music. Poems serve as fanfares and anthems to help us see and remember what is important. While there is no necessary connection between form and content, almost all poems seem to take the form of witness, a testimonial that says I was here, and this is what I learned.

Robert Morgan

Penny Dyer

Penny Dyer is the recipient of the 2007 Oberon Poetry Prize and the 2006 Louisiana Literature Prize for Poetry. Her work also appears in *Original Sin: The Seven Deadlies Come Home to Roost, SouthernReader, Poems Niederngasse, SouthLit, Arsenic Lobster, Dogwood, Oberon, New Millennium Writings and Narrative.* Penny writes in several genres and is at work on a poetry collection, *Awaiting the Fall of Babylon,* and a novel, *How Sweet the Sound.* Her poem "Summer Storm, 1963" was nominated for a Pushcart Prize.

Fingerprints

Instead, look at the painting so close
you can't see it.
Not the image the artist willed onto the bleached
canvas skeleton. Forget what you see, what you think
he meant you to see.

Instead, see the skin
stained in colored oils
not unlike the cleft above your left breast,
an earlobe, maybe the tender flesh behind a knee.

Look too, at the pigment flaking
green above a gold, brush-stroked autumn,
the dry craze on a stretched cloth
like the crackled lines on the backs of your hands.

Look too, at your child's face
lined in a parchment portrait of someone
you wanted to be.
See where the paint flecks off
in tiny dismal pieces down around the sycamore's hips,
like the fierce sweat of an autumn war, or
the sound of blood.

Look at your fingertips,
or the plowed fields of your palms.
Everything man touches,
the shined marble of museum floors,
rhombuses of wiped windows,
the swept sidewalk of your neighbor's home—
all of them, if you look close enough
are matched fingerprints.

The Way Anemones Lie

I missed you on Saturday
watching out my back door
though the undulation of salt marsh grass
told me where you were. Locusts
put in their own two cents
and so I left them to themselves–
too much talk annoyed me.
But out my front door was no better,
the Nandina blushing with the breezy gossip,
listening to the pea-gravel's undertone
beneath my slander of sandals. The mailbox
gaped its slack jaw in empty fiction.
Mockingbirds repeated alibis like Hail Marys.
Even the Day Lilies nodded–
they were all so quick to defend you.
I didn't believe them, either.

After the Morning

after Stephen Spender's *The Generous Days*
…And sidelong looks at him as though she thought
His glance might hide the gleam she sought–
He would run up to her…

–Stephen Spender

Days pass in acute angles.
Meager hours proscribed in degrees.
Breaths measured
on a scale, found wanting.

After those *generous days*,
only waiting remains full,
the watercolor sunset a blanched crimson,
the dusky walked path,
shadowed stones on tender feet,
tender hands that still touch.

In the lightless pale, *sidelong glances*
are other than consummate,
narrow segments between halted words,
sentences of unsaid promises.
Pleasantries as if strangers.

The laces of themselves, done up.
Frayed edges, unraveled seams threaten.
That *cold thing* he is,
the brooch's open clasp.

A Bequest of Constellations

One winter night you'll be heating your baby's bottle
and remember how we danced a hoedown
in our cold kitchen to Guy Clark's Texas Cookin'
or you'll hum a song you heard me sing once
—long time passing.

That will be years yet,
you sectioned off and completely
risen in your own piece of dough
but it's begun now, already goes forward
with you longing new towels, sheets,
your Granny's old table, your own toothpaste
with its life squeezed out on the white sink.

Years yet, months saved like allowance
until you might ask me for a recipe
or the name of our once neighbor
which you can't quite recall but
must remember, need to remember
in a kind of dead reckoning
to fix your position. All so cliché, I know.

You'll find some reference point to begin it,
maybe the day you first locked the lock of a diary
or the day you told me to go to hell
and I said I'd been there before and didn't
much like it but hey, feel free, to each his own.

And time will pass and go forward–this the same thing,
adding and subtracting negative and positive numbers
the way you could, precocious at four.
But later, when we are each reduced like fractions
to our least common denominators, the constellations
will have moved with the seasons,
and we will have traveled too, decimal by decimal,
light-years.
Out your kitchen window look, the night sky, look
the Big Dipper, there, Cassiopeia, Orion, there.
Familiar stars, just where they should be.

Summer Storm 1963

It's June, and the corn has begun to spear;
the house smells of matches
gone out—wet newspaper and sulfur.
Rain ticks in the gutter, reminiscent
of a carbine's clicking, and he remembers,
as he examines his hands, another summer,
the uneasy island: gray rings of orbiting ships.
Smoldering lagoons.
A slate sky with nothing written on.

That February summer, which seemed
all wrong, his hands were taut and smooth.
They were not at fault.
There was the sound of stones skipped across water.
A red sluice of one stream into another.
Then the rain began.

Now, even with the lamp gone out, he can
read the fortune in his palms, the lifelines
curling around his thumbs, and he wonders:
is atonement the longer or shorter?

As the days rust, he remembers how his knees
worked the ground, the taste of copper its own
Eucharist, the monsoon's baptism.
He keeps these wounds in a parcel
in his pocket. When it rains,
he fingers the frayed creases.

Outside the storm pummels the house.
The sweat of it spatters the sidewalk and craters
the straight mounds of a black garden. Every flaw
the rain finds exhumes a buried root.
Tomorrow he will kneel between the furrows,
cover again the gentle seedlings,
as he ponders the fold of his hands.
He considers how easily the tender fall.

Penny Dyer

Cutting My Name in the Tree

A few hundred yards through the woods
my father is young again–his bent arms swinging,
his glance back at us like someone else's
father–hurry up you two.

His careful step across the muddy creek
but ours less so; we make a mess of it
wet and ground-sucked, my only shoes spoiled.

We follow him to where the cabin once stood
and he becomes himself again,
hands pocketed and eyes measuring the wrecked timbers
as if remembering how he built it
or if he could do it again.

Let's Pretend, we say and wall our playhouses
with autumn leaves, make believe
our husbands wear black suits
and carry briefcases, picket-fence neighbors
grilling Saturday hotdogs. We were wives
in aprons–no big stretch, then abandon
it all to make a game of hiding,
Ponce de Leon searching for the fountain of youth
and finding it here, right here, on this creek.

My father watches the scenes play out.
He sits on his haunches, letting his jackknife
whittle away his past. He carves our initials
on the Poplar tree, his last mark on this land,
and ours. When it's time to walk back to our future,
my father tells us to lie
about our ruined clothes, not our fault, not his.

Awaiting the Fall of Babylon

It was an attic where I once kept
watch for the end of the world,
not a basement.
Not a bunker or fallout shelter.
Instead the slanted eaves pointed to God
and in spring,
the dogwoods crucifixed their white
crosses just beneath the window.

My sisters, skeptics to catastrophe,
slept secure in their quilted cocoons.
They did not believe in the invisible,
the plutonium wind that crept through the
oak trees, Santa Claus, Jesus or germs.

But I was a Believer
who lay wrapped in my own patchwork shroud,
pretending hell did not exist. In its place I saw
blinding clouds of fire,
walls of wind, always the wind.

On an October morning I raised the window
and leaned against its open sash. Below dogwood
berries glistened like drops of Christ's blood
at Gethsemane. There, as in that garden, I prayed
while I waited for the Lord's second coming.
The breath of God hovered.

Come to Nothing

I wish my soul were larger than it is.
                              —Andrew Hudgins

Maybe somehow at night I lose a little
with every even breath. A mote or fleck
gone unnoticed like dust in a dark room,
a room without sunbeams. Two micrograms,
less than that, a body's weight loss
someone once measured
at someone else's last gasp.

Hard to say.
There are doors in my lungs where air
comes and goes, tunnels leaking blood
with my heart's beat. If I prick a finger,
does some seep out?

Skin sealed with lotion, cracked lips.
Valleys of dry bones a–scriptures bear
this out. Such life as I find I feed
the best food, towel its wet feet,
forgive its indiscretions, line its pretty cage.
It's patient. It can wait. When I sleep, it finds
a way out with every dream, every nightmare.

Last of the Tribe

Standing before the open casket
all that was left were these last two brothers
each with his arms linking the other's waist.
We wondered–how they had done this before,
losing each other in foregone conclusions?

Years of Sunday afternoons the six of them,
as if in a waiting room, had lingered
on their mother's porch smoking
their Winstons, cradling hidden beers
within crooked elbows, then one after another
snuffed out their cigarettes
with each called name.

Fifty in our family marks the beginning
of old age–the jokes about retirement,
or the lottery win that affords
a cemetery plot with a river view.
Then this day, a Sunday
or a day that seems like one,

when we all dress for church
and pay our respects at the altar
of an open box. Close as close,
shoulder to nodded head
my uncle tells his brother
One of us has to do this again.

Humor Me

In the night I talk to the dead. It's easier when the world
is not so taken over by sound and light, when the
underworld
seems closer. Sometimes during the day I know
they are at my elbow–say when I am folding clothes,
or just beyond the door when I finish my bath,
or rolling dice against the curb at the next turned street.
You've seen them, too, out of the corner of your eye.
Then you blink.
It's easier in the dark. Less slippery.

I ask them if it's true about expanding galaxies.
Or whether time is a particle that gets bigger,
like a cosmic snowball. They love it
when I ask such questions. These are the kinds
of things they get a kick out of.
This is what I say: tell me the future. Tell me what it's like
to die.
Tell me the next lottery numbers and I'll make it worth
your while.
Tell me what music really is.

They explain that in the light of a snow-burdened tree
dusk hangs suspended. Can I close my eyes and still
see its afterimage, they ask me. Do I remember
the tune my brother whistled.
What color is it, they want to know.

In Absentia

Thunder, the sullen afternoon,
low, expansive clouds and summer heat
shifting into dusk,
pine trees groaning their loss.
Rain typing strange letters
into the eaves of the house.
Then crickets or locusts or some other creature.
It's all some kind of message,
words draining into the downspout,
the insect-language.
Porch lights, a familiar beacon.
I could almost be home.
But mother is not there,
nor my father or brother, nor anyone
who stroked my hair or told me
of light streaming from heaven,
all storms stilled after an old, old story.

The Dance

Rage deafens your ears.
How do you hear the music?
There was once a song
moving within our feet, but
it is other than that now.

Memoriam

It must be some other place
where you may have picnicked
with a lover, a park green and cool
sunsetting your back-spilled hair
against a grassy sky.

There may be a memory of your elbow's
angled curve against the damp ground,
or an afternoon slanting through
colonnades of old elms.

You recall row houses, iron-fenced courtyards
that distanced you from the fountains there,
how the charmed gates unclenched
their fisted hinges for you
and you locked them carefully back
pretending them yours.

You even remember the price of bricks
on the day the street was cobbled,
any price you remember will do—
and there's an ingrained intuition
urging your right hand to post a letter
to the mailbox on the corner.

Today looks like a grainy photograph.
Pigeons descend whirling to the plaza
below your hotel window. You see
the movement of homeless men
to the sanctity of shadows.

Penny Dyer

This is not the city you meant to visit.
Maybe what you wished for lies buried
beneath the park's new white flowers.
Maybe within your hands is an old map
overwritten in sepia, creased filigrees
of fading ink unfolding,
tracing your lifeline
to some other place than this.

Heat Lightning

August. From every pore the earth's sweat clings;
even Wind has unbuttoned his collar.
Trees fan themselves wearily with green.
Winter's page turned so long ago
it is fiction, the book's cover faded
in the sun, unreadable. No one remembers
its title. Clouds brood with temper, growl
like dreamful dogs. But nothing really moves.
Then drops pock against the house.
A sprinkle, then nothing more.
This is the way faith works,
heat lightning, the sky lit, then dark,
then lit again.

Dining with the Dead

We've packed a picnic, spread out
an old quilt at the feet of our ancestors,
sipped our coffee. My sisters sit
ankles-crossed. We visit with intention,
to bury our brother's ashes,
instead pull weeds, discard faded
plastic roses–small ceremonies
of the living for the dead.

This cemetery stubbles the hill
like an old man's sparse beard.
We read headstones as if each
was someone suddenly recognized
–the way you meet a person you've missed
for a long time. It takes a minute to know
them again, to remember whether the uncle
was that one's father or another's or no,
just someone you thought you knew.

People die so gradually
–like the guy from the loading dock,
what was his name? Or the old woman
down the street whose front yard once blazed
with poppies. Just a vague loss of red.

We laugh at the mistakes we've made,
the silly clothes we buried our mother in,
the kind she wouldn't have been caught dead
wearing, how we thought sandwiches
would make this easier.
Our brother waits, taking up his own space.
As when we were children, we ignore him.

Penny Dyer

The three of us are here, listening
for words no one says. My older sister lies back,
looks at the black clouds gathering.
Today, we can't do it.
Does he belong with the other names,
we wonder, do they call to him?
Do we talk to drown out what we don't
want to hear, all the voices here but ours,
too noisy, too much, too soon?

The Good Girl

Classroom

Dick and Jane lorded it over us,
over me, Jane's crisp pink dress
never crushed in civil defense drills
beneath her desk, and Dick's smile
never lost, always holding Sally's hand.
But mine, knuckle-white and empty,
covered my ears while the siren
screamed and screamed. And screamed.

> *Some glad morning when this life is o'er,*
> *I'll fly away.*
> *To a home on God's celestial shore,*
> *I'll fly away.*

Library

Biographies streaked blue and brown canvases,
wet paintings that moved me, that I moved within.
From every open book ghosts stirred
to speak to someone like me,
the one no one missed at recess.
I heard what they told me,
mouthed their words as I read.
Quietly now, they said to me.
We have chosen you.
Hope, they shouted.

> *I'll fly away, O Glory,*
> *I'll fly away.*
> *When I die, Hallelujah, by and by,*
> *I'll fly away.*

Penny Dyer

Gymnasium

We fledglings formed our straight
and narrow lines alphabetically
on the varnished gym floor,
my Easter Mary Janes squeaking out
the Lord's Prayer with every black mark.
The doctor listened to our sparrow-chests,
bade us open our bird-mouths to receive
the living Eucharist of polio's crystal drop.
My face reflected small moons
in my shoes' patent leather. The principal penciled
our names in his book of life. But only the janitor
would blot out our trespasses.

> *When the shadows of this life have flown,*
> *I'll fly away.*
> *Like a bird thrown, driven by the storm,*
> *I'll fly away.*

Playground

I feared what fell from the sky.
Softballs were guided missiles, the pendulum
of tetherball a trebuchet. Nor did I possess
what *the others* would accept in lieu:
A father after whose name followed degrees
as if a thermometer rising, a mother
who placed pretty what-nots on polished
shelves, who gave to the poor as if
they were not her own neighbors.
I laced rosaries of lanyards.

Penny Dyer

Just a few more weary days and then,
I'll fly away.
To a land where joy shall never end,
I'll fly away.

Bay of Pigs 1962

My first school medal stamped out
my name in tin, breached the sea
of my dark hair to circle my neck.
The rich girls tucked theirs beneath
starchy crinolines.

At the end of the world
mine glimmered atop
my hand-me-down dress:
Look at me, it said; this is my name.
Who I am. Here. I am *here*.

Publication Credits

Fingerprints – won second place and was first published in the Chattanooga Writers' Guild Anthology, 2004

The Way Anemones Lie; Summer Storm, 1963 – first published in *Arsenic Lobster*, Summer 2006

Awaiting the Fall of Babylon – first published in *Southlit.com*, April 2006; subsequently published in *The Chattanooga Writer* and *New Millennium Writings*, 2007-2008

(Some of the poems herein appear in slightly altered forms from the originals.)

Bill Brown

Bill Brown, who grew up in Dyersburg, Tennessee, is the author of five collections of poetry, three chapbooks and a writing textbook on which he collaborated with Malcolm Glass. Late Winter, a collection of poems, was released in spring 2008 by Iris Press. His newest collection, The News Inside, was released by Iris Press in 2010. During the past twenty years, he has published hundreds of poems and articles in college journals, magazines and anthologies. In 1999, Brown wrote and co-produced the Instructional Television Series, Student Centered Learning, for Nashville Public Television. He holds a degree in history from Bethel College and graduate degrees in English from the Bread Loaf School of English, Middlebury College and George Peabody College. Since 1983, Brown directed the writing program at Hume-Fogg Academic High School in Nashville. He retired from Hume-Fogg in May 2003 and accepted a part time lecturer's position at Peabody College of Vanderbilt University. In 1995, the National Foundation for Advancement in the Arts named him Distinguished Teacher in the Arts. He has been a Scholar in Poetry at the Bread Loaf Writers Conference, a Fellow at the Virginia Center for the Creative Arts, a two-time recipient of Fellowships in poetry from the Tennessee Arts Commission, and twice the recipient of the Smith-Corona Award for entering the best student writing in the National Scholastic Writing Awards. He and his wife Suzanne live in the hills of Robertson County with a tribe of cats.

Telling the Bees

(Mountain legend says when a death occurs,
a member of the family is sent to tell the bees,
or harm will come.)

That week Luke Hughes was found
two days gone with his throat torn.
Grand Sally saw the new moon
through a window pane and the bees
came in my dream. Thousands spread
like a giant carpet flying Luke
away to Jesus. I woke with a start,
dressed and left the house, ordained.
Up Cub Creek I stopped to drink,
dipped the tin cup and saw my neck
distort with pain. Nobody knew
what tore Luke's throat.
Around each laurel corner I paused
to listen, and imagined every space
as a man's shape marked by root and stone.
On the high meadow the bee boxes
greeted me like temples carved white
against the blue-green grass.
I turned each to the right three times
and stood before them proclaiming
Lukas G. Hughes is dead by the power
of a new moon and Sally Brown sent
me here to let you know.
The bee buzz grew around me
and the blood of Luke Hughes
was harvested and turned to wax.

Night Song

(For Robert)

All night trees rained
leaves against the roof.
Hickory, maple and oak
palmed and scraped
wood and tin, combed
the air like ghost hands
freed from the hands of men
who grieved with hands.

And in the illogic of half sleep
the side of my brain which understands
my heart heard the sound of the leaves
as they tossed across the night.

I have lived among these trees for years
and we have felt the sky's weight
heavy on our seed. We are passengers
on this gracious rock which circles
a dying star.

And some nights I take this on faith,
that the same glue which holds
my life in balance, allows
the earth to fly the moon
like a kite and scatters these leaves
through this night, homeward.

On a Park Bench in Heaven

On a park bench in heaven
my grandparents sit staring
through all that holiness
which glimmers, they think,
like freezing rain on winter trees.

They were pleased to be here
at first, flattered to be taken
despite all their Sunday plowing.
The pearly gates are just fine
my grandmother says, but
she would trade the lot for a tin of snuff.

My Grandfather would sell
his soul for a pocket watch,
he's tired of asking every saint
who flies by what time it is.

All this gold and silver remind
them of the dining room
at the Jackson Holiday Inn.
What they really miss is the smell
of honeysuckle or the way
woodland violets circle star trillium
like a wedding quilt in the spring.

We've been here twenty years
my grandfather says
and to date, no funerals,
no sick friends, no floods,
no droughts, no nips of sour mash
at the general store
on Saturday afternoons.

And harp music day and night,
not one angel flat-picks
or sings a whisky tenor.
In the pickup glove
compartment of his heart,
he wonders if hell wasn't
a little more like Tennessee.

Talking to You Asleep

Searching the drawer for matching socks
I watched you sleeping and
it dawned on me how much
I like cutting tall weeds in the orchard
while you mow the yard.
The orchard's five rows
of morning shadows
move in strange regiment
through the day.
Listen, we have fought
twenty years successfully,
sometimes for, sometimes
against, oftentimes
just for the sake of fighting,
and I still smile when
you get up in the dark
and trip over my hiking boots.
When you crawl over me
to get on your side of the bed,
you pay me back
with your sharp knees.
We have five degrees, two cats,
and an old farmhouse.
In the morning quiet
your hair still falls in barmaid tangles
against your pillow.
The only movement is through
the window by your head,
wind breaking orchard shadows when
leaves dapple them with light.

Foolish Hands

A month after your death
I caught my fingers
dialing you at work.
I stared at my hand
holding the phone.
Hands can be so foolish.
I have awakened from a dream
to find them screaming
in the dark, the hands
that held your hands,
palmed your back,
affectionately glanced
your shoulder.
But it's not all their fault,
the little scholars have
such brutal memories.
They wish that they were
just dumb clubs used
to bang the lonely walls
of our house, or simple masks
to hide my face in shame.
The hands that held your hands,
and straightened the hair
around your neck.
Something sensitive about the tips
of the fingers let them remove
an eyelash from the corner of your eye,
or squeeze a splinter from your foot.

Now these clumsy digits
might make better wings,
the way they flail the air.
I'll have to lock them in my pockets,
mitten their mindless fidgets
or they'll give away my pain.
Now that's an idea.
Hands could give away my sorrow.

Early This Morning

The sheet pulled
away and your scar glowed
like a crescent moon
in the quiet light.
My first impulse
was to cover you
but found myself studying
how flesh and skin heal,
how tiny tracks disappear
to form a symbol like
primitive cave paintings:
a bone tool like a scythe,
the rounded slope of elk.
What would an anthropologist
say about this tiny icon;
that it signifies genetic curse,
something sinister in our world
that spirits female cells awry.

Bill Brown

Does it stand for survival, shame,
bravery, fear, as you sit in
a warm tub examining
your own tissue, searching
for the smallest lump.
You stir and I tuck the sheet
around your shoulder, careful
to cover this pale halo
in the safety of our room.
How will you tell me
if there is a next time:
over coffee, in the car
on the way to work?
When is there a right
moment, though we have
slept three decades
skin to skin?

The Right to Drown

(For Roger)

In the past there was protection
against drowning.
Sailors bought a baby's caul
from shrewd midwives
and kept this precious membrane
in a box locked away
like a fetus breathing
through its mother's blood.

You must have known this could happen
every time you kneeled in a canoe
to learn another river.
There is integrity in risk.
Yesterday a hitchhiker saw
my whitewater paddle
and asked if I had ever known you,
said you had drowned in the Watauga Gorge.

I wouldn't let the messenger tell me
how they found you or whether you lips
were blue. I only hoped
that when the soft bubbles in your lungs
gave way to a flood
your fingers held like river kelp
to rock, your feet kicked
the cold water you must face
in your long sleep.

Snake Story

(For Robert)

When Danny stopped the truck,
the rattlesnake lay in the gravel
five feet long, shivering like
a fevered arm. Someone had
cut the head and rattles.
It'll make a belt," he said,
"hold the tail and I'll skin it clean."
30 years of fearing snakes
started in my stomach, climbed
my spine, scale by scale,
like a copperhead bellying up
the kitchen window.
I was holding snake meat,
mealy and loose, but its muscles
still tightened a figure eight
as Danny's knife slit the anus.
He peeled the skin inside out
away from serpent flesh
and I had to hold tight
with both hands. My fingers
pressed knobby tail bone,
and felt the spinal vertebrae
testify a million years
of belly crawling, past legs,
no shoulders, just long slinking
snake evolution swallowing
warm blooded mammals whole.

Suddenly Danny's fingers slipped
and four feet of skinned snake
coiled up my arm like a bed spring from hell.
The beheaded nub struck my cheek
and I had to smile to keep
from dying. On that mountain road
I slung that chain of meat toward the sky
like a bola hunting God,
and when it fell, a wingless angel,
around a blossomed dogwood limb,
I swear it moved.

Third World Primer

Children, say these words clearly:

WOMB BOMB TOMB

Place the palm of your hand to your lips,
close your eyes and say WOOOMB,
blowing the warm air between your fingers.
Using both hands, put your thumbs together,
then your forefingers. Form a triangle
over your navel, feel the shape
try to pull you back inside.

Now, say BOMB BOMB BOMB BOMB.

There can never be just one.
Ready? Quickly crawl under your work tables,
kneel on your knees and place your head
to the floor. Cover your head with your hands
and begin to scream until everyone is screaming.
This means you are alive.

Without getting up, roll over on your back
and when the light is out, shut your eyes
and imagine you feel the wooden table
close around you. Place the tip of your tongue
to the roof of your mouth, breathe deeply
and very slowly say
        TOOOMB.

My Brother's Hands, 1964

My oldest brother home from med school,
our family took iced tea into the backyard
beside the wet weather creek to enjoy
the oak broken sun of Sunday. To my joy
and my mother's jitters, my brother
lifted a rat snake that crawled
up to rest its head on his shoe.
With the gentle precision of his hands
that would one day be a surgeon's,
he let my sister and me touch its skin
as the snake roped between his fingers.

What I never told came late that afternoon.
I crept back by the stream to find the snake,
but boys from the Baptist picnic found it first,
and steeped in their parent's lore,
stoned it into oblivion. With sticks,
so as not to touch it, they hung the snake
on the Hanson's fence, perhaps
to ward off evil or bring rain
to the desert in their hearts.

Within a year my brother's hands
bandaged soldiers in Vietnam,
as my mother wrung her hands in prayer,
and mine were busy banging out
protest songs on a Sears guitar.
At night I dreamed the physician's hands
holding a serpentine staff instead
of a crucifix, blessing the foreheads
of boys he couldn't save.

Bill Brown

The Names of Hats

An aigrette is a hat decorated
with egret tail feathers. Looking up
a word in the dictionary, I saw
a picture of a French woman
wearing one. I thought of the egret roost
outside of my home town.
It was a glorious sight, hundreds
of white birds gathered in trees
at the edge of a swamp,
carrying on mating rituals.
Of course, a housing development,
with a name like Quail Ridge,
was built close by. The swamp
was drained, the egrets killed
or driven off to stop histoplasmosis.
Twenty years ago, I taught school
with a man who had the malady.
He contracted the disease
on a Saturday outing
when he entered a boarded up
train station filled with pigeons.
He was a bitter little man
who chain smoked and complained
of ignorant students who wouldn't read.
He sued the train company
and waited years to win
enough money to stop teaching.
It never happened. Last May,
my wife and I went fishing
at Reelfoot Lake. It was a day
filled with the surprise of egrets.
In territorial feeding disputes,
they chased each other from lily pads

to snake grass to cypress roots,
squawking, flashing snow white wings.
I don't know how most hats
get their names, or, if human fates
and birds were reversed, whether egrets wouldn't
adorn their hats with my wife's golden hair,
just that on page 27 of my dictionary,
the word aigrette started memories
that led to stories that led me here.

Damaged Child, Shack Town, Elm Grove, Oklahoma, 1936
From a photograph by Dorothea Lange

You stand against the muted grays of aged tin and stone.
Barn shadows almost hide bruised cheeks and arms.
A handsome quality frames your face, heavily browed eyes

narrowed into a thin defiant gaze: a look that says you'll
bust someone's balls if they're not careful. It's hard to say
if the shirt you wear, with one strap tied in a square knot

on your right shoulder, was once a man's sleeveless,
or from a woman's cotton shift. I've seen children
with your stare, who know more than their years suppose.

They have stood in containment camps from Palestine
to Rwanda, and on city streets from Memphis to Los
Angeles.
I won't make stories of how your mother clutched you

to her breast to shield you from your father's drunken
breath,
nor imagine tender moments when your grandpa taught you
how to fish, nor shiver at what night's darkness brought.

You wear the slight grin of the proud and hungry,
too smart not to know a rotten world when you've
found one, and, cruelly, too smart not to dream.

From the Night Porch

The silhouette of Snow Ridge,
trees tossing in windshears
from a coming storm,
reminds me of a flight

from L.A. home to
Tennessee: the jerking plane,
the bolts of lightning
by the wing. A woman

asked to close my window
as if fear of crashing
would be lessened by
what she could not see.

Her voice was like my
sister's, soft and direct,
who once told me when
I was small and scared:

"Darkness is your friend,
a twin you have to match
the cave you have inside."
Listen:

memory is easily broken
by the sound of trees,
the sound of trees
erased by memory

The dark ridge above
the creek is rich
with both.
A flash of lightning,

I count
one Mississippi,
two Mississippi, three –
then thunder:

storms are like the future,
three miles away,
closing fast.
The cave I have inside
is opened by the wind,
like the dark ridge
surprised by lightning
and the rush of leaves.

Many times I stand
on this porch
to watch the storms fill up
with trees

and hear my sister's voice
in the night
speak of darkness
as a friend.

This memory
without fear
webs me to the night
beauty of this land.

Thanksgiving 1956

On that angry Thanksgiving,
my sullen uncle drank bourbon
early morning and in a struggle
got revenge against my grandmother
for birthing his wife,
for his own twisted fate.

While Granny prepared dinner
for twenty, he removed her hens
from the egg shack and buried them,
one by one, up to the neck
in a row as straight as a furrow
in her garden.

Before dinner he invited the whole clan
out behind the barn where he said,
"This is what I think of Thanksgiving."
He started the push mower
and, while we stood in disbelief,
mowed the heads down.

My grandmother stared at the jumble
of clicking beaks and blinking eyes,
at the ground which looked like twenty
pink crawdad holes sucking and gurgling air.
As she stared at the sky for a sign,
a stern indifference crossed her face.

With the tight-lipped grin she had borne
past one depression, two wars,
three dead sons, a husband
and a number of slighter heartbreaks,
she looked my uncle square in the face
and whispered,
"So?"

The Calling

Something calls above the tops of trees:
not exactly the wind, or crows having

their morning disagreement; not my dead
whose voices I remember like the smell

of biscuits, the taste of molasses and butter;
not would-be lovers and their lonely fingers,

but a clear calling, one of October blue
and crisp air, one of heavy dew dripping

from gum and maple like rain; not lowland fog
that whispers to grass; not my childhood friends

who, living or dead, still dwell in the land
of leaf piles and trees, complaining

to the sky when their mothers call them home.
Not a song, but a calling like the circle

a hawk makes or the dull moon in daylight,
or the fire and purple rings after looking

at the sun. I strain to hear the voice
of bright unopened moments, but how can

I listen to what was almost said: the sound
of a girl's hair that never touched my pillow,

the poems I forgot in some airport in Kansas,
the words I imprisoned until my father died.

Siasconset Time

-after Eavan Boland

Time is measured by the pace of waves;
skate eggs, whelk chains, and seaweed
mark high tide. She reads Tao on the sand,
presses primrose and yellow scotch broom,

while he casts for blues off the point.
Later, darkness hides an inch of wine
left in a glass, her hair against his cheek,
footprints snaking tide and sand along the beach.

Words get lost on islands; what was meant,
remembered best by lips, restful sleep,
the tips of fingers. In the morning, fog hides
the house, the hamlet, all but the ocean's roar.

Back in the city, he recalls the endless swells
stretching a dark sea larger than a continent.
She dreams a bright line sweeping across the shore,
the surprise of roses when the fog lifts.

Solstice

To learn about light
I sit on the porch and watch
winter trees filter sun.

I never know how to greet the silence,
except to breathe quietly, monitor
heart thumps in my temples.

This morning blood and sun
are part of the mystery
alchemists ignored.

The hawk in its lonely circle knows.
The crow tells its shadow.
I'm taking notes on milkweed,

how the pods creep open
and loose angels into light.
Monarch butterflies feed

on those toxic plants,
teach birds not to eat
bright wings. Everything

sublime isn't deadly
and that's another season.
Today is early December.

The sky, a deeper blue, floats
toward the longest night
when the pulse slows,

when light is more need
than blessing, when things
that glitter are almost gold.

Worship

This morning I open the wood stove
and hear something escape the chimney.
Maybe the ghost of last May,
a month too warm for burning,
when we built a roaring fire
and left the doors open.
There's a spirit in a stove.
When I was twenty, I scoffed
at myths like the hearth god.
At fifty I'll practice any ritual
born from simple human need,
god of morning coffee and Sunday papers,
god of lazy love making, wine and old books;
god of tilling, planting and harvesting.
I won't recognize the god of television,
videos, or cellular phones,
but the god of old tractors,
handmade tools, raking leaves,
and sweeping the porch.
Praise be to the god of sheets billowing
like sails in the sun and the dank god
of storm cellars, spidery and safe.
I kneel willingly to the god
of stirring soup and kneading bread,
to all gods of needful work.
So this morning after hearing
the stove god haunt the chimney,
I kindle the first fall fire
to all the gods of necessity
who keep us fed and warm,
and to the gods of little pleasures
who help us be kind.

Black Widow

Some things you're not supposed to own.
I found her at Grandmother's house
under a rock, black plump body
and crab-like legs, her red hourglass
keeping time. I coaxed her into
a mason jar, added grass, and hid
her in a pouch. My brother's book
said that she held death in her fangs.
I could shake her if I wanted. Don't
pretend that you've never desired
to possess a certain danger,
harbor your prize from others,
take it from its vault and jiggle it,
some control of what we inherit at birth
(hourglass and fat darkness).
I've heard of soldiers who smuggle
live grenades, bayonets, human ears,
and keep them hidden in attic boxes
until they die, leaving their shrapnel
for others to find. I carried the hidden jar,
and when I dropped it and it broke in town,
my father saw the spider and shook
his head. He took it on a newspaper
into the alley and let it live
as I scooped up the glass.
My father was a simple, gentle man
with like solutions. "Be careful what
you hide and play with," he said.

Publication Credits

Telling the Bees – *first published in Cumberland Poetry Review*, later included in *What the Night Told Me*. (Mellon Poetry Press)

Night Song – first published in *Poems of Nature and the Sacred*, later included in *What the Night Told Me*. (Mellon Poetry Press)

On a Park Bench in Heaven – first published in *Pikestaff Forum*, later included in *What the Night Told Me*. (Mellon Poetry Press)

Talking to You Asleep – first published in *Negative Capability*, later included in *What the Night Told Me*. (Mellon Poetry Press).

Foolish Hands – First published in *The Southern Poetry Review*, later included in *The Art of Dying* (Sow's Ear Press)

The Right to Drown – first published in *What the Night Told Me*. (Mellon Poetry Press).

Snake Story – first published in *Snake Nation Review*, later included in *What the Night Told Me*. (Mellon Poetry Press).

Third World Primer – first published in *Number One*, later included in *What the Night Told Me*. (Mellon Poetry Press)

My Brother's Hands, 1964 – first published in *The Literary Review*, later included in *Tatters* (March Street Press)

The Names of Hats – first published in *Tar River Poetry*, later included in *Tatters* (March Street Press)

Damaged Child, Shack Town, Elm Grove, Oklahoma, 1936 – first published in *Smartish Pace*, later included in *Tatters* (March Street Press)

From the Night Porch – first published in *The Literary Review*, later included in *The Art of Dying* (Sow's Ear Press)

Thanksgiving 1956 – first published in *Number One*, later included in *The Art of Dying* (Sow's Ear Press)

The Calling – first published in *Poems and Plays*, later included in *Yesterday's Hay* (Pudding House Press) and the news inside (Iris Press, 2010)

Siasconset Time – first published in *Visions International*, later included in *Yesterday's Hay* (Pudding House Press) and the news inside (Iris Press, 2010)

Solstice – first published in *The Rambler*, later included in *Yesterday's Hay* (Pudding House Press) and the news inside (Iris Press, 2010)

Worship – first published in *The Southern Poetry Review*, later included in *Gods of Little Pleasures* (Sow's Ear Press)

Black Widow – first published in *Yesterday's Hay* (Pudding House Press) and the news inside (Iris Press, 2010)

Bruce Majors

Bruce Majors grew up in East Tennessee, graduated from Tennessee Technological University, and retired from the Tennessee Valley Authority. He has published poems in Arts and Letters, Pinesong, The Distillery, River Poets Journal, Number One, and other literary journals. His book, The Fields of Owl Roost, is an autobiographical collection of loosely-related poems that has been said to capture the eccentricity of our imperfect world. It was named first finalist in the 2005 Indie Excellence Book Awards.

Winter Sun

The fact that light is leaving,
something in the winter sun,
the angle it strikes my eyes,
the more than usual thin, pale light
or the way fields lie in thinner
light of midday, makes me sad.
Something about the equinox
I don't understand.

Maybe the way sun rims hillsides
in small patches of gold light, on snow,
around cedars, or filters through tall
sage making a musty, red-brown glow
you can almost smell.

Mostly sadness comes above me
from somewhere in air
in a hollow of thought
after light has done its work.

I lament the heaviness of winter sun
as it slants through glass
at my feet.

I lament the failing force that searches
continually through skeletons of trees
against a winter horizon
for some logic in the changing light.

I lament the passing of light, gradual
ebbing of spirit to a glimmered sunset,
subtle metamorphosis toward early sleep,
something in winter sun I don't understand.

About Snow

There are things you should know about snow
when it comes at night,

spreading a dark-white cover
over fields, illuminating breath
with what thin light is left

of the missing moon.

Snow, pressing, in pale shadows,
the light it seems to generate,
power of that light seeming to purify,
freedom of purification, to break loose
parts of myself, stuffed inside, energy,
not acceptable in ordinary light.

> . . .

In the fields, stems of Johnson grass
and wild rose briar crackle,
tiny sounds augmented by my crunching boots
through icy stillness.
Every other thing lies buried
in deep gloom, purified in the prefrontal
cortex or a mouse's bed or some other
secret place.

> . . .

I won't tell you I have been changed
by the magic of snow
or the world has been changed
or even one field mouse.
I can only say I walk these nights,
feet frozen, hands numb,
snow falling on my hair, shoulders,
hoping it may release the burning
grip of things a heart can't let go,
resolve mistakes that can't be recalled...

Perhaps, in time,
when snow falls, again,
at night.

Bruce Majors

Passing by Pleasant Hill Baptist Church at Dusk

A sinner in a Ford truck sucking on Pabst
Blue Ribbon
half drunk, not half in love with anything,
I wonder
what the Lord must think.

Tires rip and crack the graveled road,
offer jolted prayer on my behalf to a God
who does not entirely believe in me.
I don't even know what prayer really is:

Cicadas choiring through pines,
an owl's hoot over a shadowed lake,
or I, stranded on uncertain knees to beg
forgiveness of sins I don't remember.

My old truck brakes at the ramp.
I stand upright in spirit, wholly lighted,
baptized in moonlight,
slide a john boat into the dark waters of absolution…
The only salvation I may ever know.

Flying Like Angels

We made John's Place an icon,
Pabst Blue Ribbon like sacred wine,
a watering hole for the lost.
Somehow we always got back to school.

Minds blew at the edge of knowledge,
psychedelic dynamo, free love time,
leaning toward darkness or light
—freedom hard.

José Garcia wore ringlets of love
in army green, stepped on a land mine,
came home in a box.
Didn't make it back to school.

We thought smoke-filled days, liquid nights
would never end—now it seems like,
what's the song? Purple Haze…
But we were cool in that purple mist

driving the dark side of the road,
flying like angels going nowhere
in a blue-flowered yellow van
and the red door painted black.

Planting Buckwheat

Night swarms with rain,
no wind.
The seed I put out will benefit,
    and birds,
will have much to sing about
    in fall.

Nothing comes of the stringy buckwheat
    toward beauty.
It doesn't flower,
not an aromatic crop,

    sturdy,
like the ancestors who brought it here
beating out time with axes and plows.
    A sustainer,
no nonsense brown stalk,
burly pod with stamina enough
    to multiply for ages.

Sometimes determination is all that's needed
    rows not defined
    edges not clearly marked
seeds grow toward the sun
without knowing why
this is the way life should be lived.

Hauling a Load of Hay, 1952

Papa stood on the very front of the flat bed wagon, his mules, Jude and
Kate, easing the wagon through the crackly stubble
of hayfield. He held lathered lines steady so they moved gently, back and
forth across the mules' backs. Sweat on Papa's neck glistened.

Wagon loaded, we headed to the barn to stack hay. I don't know if Papa
noticed pretty things–maybe ancient work and pretty things were the
same to him. Being there in those days
of gentleness and fire felt like cool water through a sieve of green leaves
and ice.

The wagon crunched down a tree-lined lane paved with yellow ridge-
gravel, old fencerow on each side. Past orchard, the mules stopped at
the well under English oaks. Water cool and sweeter than any wine I've
tasted since. Down on one knee, we tilted the bucket, drank big gulps,
sloshing out both sides of mouths, wetting shirts, quenching thirsts so
completely it was the water of life made sweeter by soft scents of nearby
honeysuckle, clover. An oasis in time.

Papa leaned back against the well, closed his eyes, maybe slept. I lay on
my back, stared at speckled light penetrating branches. A slight breeze
rattled leaves and shifted light like time. I never awaken from that dream.

Prozac Dream

I don't know, I said when she asked me
to describe the feeling. A dark room,
maybe, dread of the next few
minutes…not happy for no reason.

With Prozac and Paxil
the monsters hid in tremors, bad
dreams, night sweats.
For a while.

But then, I don't know,
something I meant to do
got left out,
like when you see a gray sheet
of rain slanting across
a field, the blind white eye
of some lost animal seeking shelter.

She said you keep on going.
I said there is no air in this place.

The walker in white helmet and suit
slips away like dust
in the stillness of space.
In perfect calm, he drifts away.

Bruce Majors

The slow hand of a lover
waves from behind a window,
hesitantly,
to someone leaving in rain.
Someone who is always leaving.

Nothing changes.
The tightness of space preserves everything.

Freights

A freight whines in the distance.
Diesel lungs cough black smoke rings,
lunging forward,
twisting light through trees,
midnight village of clacking wheels.

A boy lies in bed, listens.
Sounds pass along the open window,
peepers chime in like an afterthought
of green willows.

The breeze barely lifts itself,

a freight
deep in the distant silence…

harvest gold moon,

night trees,

cicada's scratchy love song to his sleepy mate.

And sleep drifts down
in the white hall of dreams
and midnight clacking of wheels.

Dark Tenor

There's a place in the woods
I go when too many voices
fill the room,

a hollow that opens
into a small glade with moon–
light burned softly, deeply
into the dark outline of trees,
low fog often settling there.

When the wind is right,
I imagine I hear the voice
of my old dead father
calling me through the dark,
whispering my name,

or it is wind sieved so fine
it becomes the semblance
of a voice,

or groanings themselves
meshed with the sound of wind
wanting to forgive the pains
of these many years. It lengthens,
whispers down the corridor
of a windy hollow, and is lost
in the rattle of leaves
somewhere behind me.

How Awful to Be Special

I noticed the darkness of the room
where it met edges of sunlight
from the window, dark border
of light across the bed.
How sunlight against darkness
made the color of straw,
light changing each object, each with
its own glow.
I thought of that picture of a gray-haired
country doctor bent over his patient,
chin in hand, deep in thought,
as if he could do something for the death
lying before him, somewhere
within him…and the miracle just above him
and how that light seemed like the light
in my father's room.
The air changed, a shifting plane,
light from the window angled
into the room, particles suspended
in the yellow glow, like moths
pulsing through candlelight.

How awful to be special,
to be the one on whom dreams depend.

Shadows, Late at Night

Out across the lake,
shaded ringlets corrugate
the moon's gaze,
dance a soft vibrato,
hushed into smoothness.

Night bugs croon
symphonic sketches.
The slight breeze, nothing more than a riffle
of ideas.

All are asleep but me.

My strange shape lurks
in milk-white shadows,
knowing secrets,
remembering vast loneliness,

ah, the vast loneliness.

Listening to My Heart Beat

Life is a breath,

a failing instant,

infinity…

A one-celled organism
whose life is complete
in a molecule of water
that evaporates on a leaf
in the morning sun,
reproduces itself
a thousand times in that mist.

Infinite life exists:

For centuries,

      years,

            seconds…

8-20-99

I went out in the fields today
among galloping horses
with wide nostrils.

They ran high circles.

I stepped deliberately,
meeting the wind
face to face,

the cat wind
that climbed behind my eyes,

coolness of clover.

Nuclear Medicine

They said I had a blockage,
maybe 2
and that I should take
325 mg of aspirin
until we knew for sure
what we were dealing with.
Then, if all is well,
go to 81 mgs,
which would do the job OK
and I could possibly
avoid a 2nd heart attack
if I exercised every day,
changed my diet,
stopped drinking so much liquor,
never smoked again,
never got excited.

The needle would not
go in the right place
though she poked and gouged
and complained that never
have I had so much trouble
getting an IV started.
I complained that neither had I.
Then the blood rushed into the vial.
A warm feeling, a treadmill,
a shot to make me feel tired.
The capillaries excitedly
did their jobs.
And the breathing and the sweat
and the modules and monitors blinked
and blinked and the neurons talked
to the morons and they told me
I was in good shape
but my heart was hard on one side.

That's because my heart has been
broken before, I said.
And we left the room, me on a rolling
table like you see in a morgue scene.
And the whirring of machines
and blinking lights and she said
I love you after the CAT scan.

And I said yes, I know.

And she said how many
blockages can you take?

And I said you don't
love me.

And she said will
your insurance pay?

And I said words are not important
now,
And this glow is probably
nuclear born,
and we shouldn't be seen together
anymore.
And the white sheet pulled over my head,
and breathing stopped,
and a trickle of blood
where the massive stick was.

Picking Blackberries

Picking blackberries was family time. It took the whole day.
Life open, no fast food stores, no interstates.
Nobody had been to the moon;
Martin Luther King and John Kennedy had not met.
All roads were bumpy,
darkness fell when lights went out.

We did things ourselves, slower,
laughed more, talked and listened, cooked and cleaned.
Men worked in the fields.
We were farmers when we could afford it.

Our white, two-story farmhouse,
set among tall oaks, box elders, cotton woods.
An old house with more souls than we knew.
The back porch L-shaped where we kids played
when it rained.
Three generations lived together,
a cistern at one end of the porch.

I imagined it the entrance to the blackberry fields,
and if we dove in we'd come up swimming
in watery fields of blackberries. Huge berries
beckoning from deep in the briary subculture of thorns.
Scratches endured for the succulent prize.

Hot pies waited in the oven warmer.
Jellies and jams from the cellar.
Cool, damp, musty cellar where watermelons cooled,
where winter was planned in canned food,
and old blue bell jars waited to be discovered.
Frogs got in but couldn't get out
or maybe they liked the dark security of constant temperature.

Too soon, sun still hot on our faces,
acorns began to fall, hummingbirds left
and blackberry briars no longer drooped with magic fruit.
We faced long days of winter to measure endurance
no longer swimming in luxurious summer.

So long laughter, so long.
Wait for us in May.
We'll be back. Wait for us.

Publication Credits

Winter Sun and About Snow – first printed in *Distillery*

Passing by Pleasant Hill Baptist Church at Dusk– forthcoming in *River Poets Journal*

Flying Like Angels – first printed in *River Poets Journal*, special edition

Planting Buckwheat – first printed in *Number One*

Hauling a Load of Hay, 1952 – first printed in *NCPS Pinesong*

Prozac Dream, Freights, Dark Tenor, How Awful It Is to Be Special, Shadows Late at Night, Listening to My Heart Beat, 8-20-99, and Nuclear Medicine – first printed in *The Fields Of Owl Roost*

Picking Blackberries – first printed in *Arts & Letters*

(Some of the poems herein appear in slightly altered forms from the originals.)

Jenny Sadre-Orafai

Jenny Sadre-Orafai's first chapbook, Weed Over Flower, was chosen for publication by Finishing Line Press. Her poetry has appeared in or is forthcoming in: Wicked Alice, can we have our ball back?, FRiGG, Plainsongs, Literary Mama, Poetry Midwest, Dash, Boxcar Poetry Review, Slant, caesura, Gargoyle, H_NGM_N, and other fine journals. Sadre-Orafai's prose has appeared in Rock Salt Plum and in the Seal Press anthology, Waking Up American. She currently serves as poetry editor for JMWW and is an Assistant Professor of English at Kennesaw State University.

Where Wedding Bands Go

I tried to sell it, tried to swallow it.
I tried to bury it in a field behind
a house that didn't belong to me.
I tried to throw it over some blue bridge
where I had once thrown a horseshoe charm.
I tried staring at it until it vanished.
I tried sliding it on my dog's tail,
hoping it would glide off her stumpy
thing and fall into hands that could
give it what it needs—a good polishing,
and a finger that wants it.

Your Death

I pretend you're dead.
I don't let them say
your name around me.
I was taught it's impolite
to talk behind a dead man's back.

I wear black four months and ten days.

I smell your clothes
one last time before
hand washing them, bagging,
and then giving them away.
I don't give your mother a thing.

I pray for what's left of you.

I stack the wedding ring, all the rings
you gave me on my right hand,
my proclamation that you are
no longer with us or like us,
the living, doing things.

I tell myself what I tell myself
to keep from going back.

Wreck

Everyone waits for it. Each strand he touched,
shorn. Set free from her soon-to-be prickled head.
Leaving the evidence on the linoleum as reminder.

They've seen it before in the movies on TV.
Cars wrecked on purpose and then set on fire.
His hand-tailored suits ride shotgun and singed.

They all wait for the smell of tobacco.
Some habit she starts that's not associated
with him. Something he won't know about.

And they listen for it. An inappropriate lover
in inappropriate places. A see-through office,
a loaded train, the toilet in an airplane.

They know it's coming already. They want
to put both hands on it. Stand witness.
Measure her before and after. Place bets.

Pushing Past

If you visit where I live now, you won't
find all my books unpacked yet. Seven boxes,
like mountains I can't climb, are slid against
the wall where someone who isn't me
would place bar stools.

Our pictures are in a box marked
THE PAST and stored in my parents' garage.
Slippery photos of Vegas in May, fountains
spraying a naïve and nice-looking married couple
grow musty beside a car that can't move without a push.

My trousseau and the charcoal portraits you drew
and I never framed lay atop old records closeted
off my porch. I open the closet door every day.
My face always stares back at me.
I dare it to run away and join the circus.

Full Circle

One weekend morning I mark
our backyard with a breadcrumb trail
while you're steeped in the shower.

The trail flares out like a comet,
a centipede curled into his death.
The symmetry is gorgeous.

As you dry off, I tell you: Leave
behind the compass, the barometer,
the metal detector. Figure it out on your own.

I guide you to the trail's mouth
and fire the emergency kit flare gun.
We needed the dramatic beginning.

My distress signal is a traitor.
It listens to itself, pings out, diving
to bury itself in a stack of leaves.

Tapping a fingernail on my father's
stopwatch hanging from my neck,
I ache for your failure. I refuse you clues.

I await your unsafe return. Without
breakfast, I imagine you hungry and weak.
I know you'll eat my desperate message.

They will name you

Clarissa.
If I concentrate hard enough
you will swallow me whole
like a snake, like I am the prey.

You and your shuffling water
on all sides. You're coming
from another county where
you made wood into woodpile.

I slide a gaudy ring on my left
middle finger. My father gave me
it when I was only ten. It was too big
for such small hands and still is.

And, since I've never seen another
ring like this one, I know that
if they find this ring, Clarissa,
in an open field when it's morning,

they will know you tried to take me
with you, but that I tasted like
an iron fist, like poison, and then like
a bronze medal going down.

What You Wanted

We could say I gave you what you wanted:
a smaller you with fists that clutch at air,
tiny nails scratching my chin. We could say
the labor was a breeze, so short, like it never happened.
That we didn't know the sex until he pushed his way out.

a smaller you, you, you, with inky curls wilting
against a soft head. That he stops crying once you unlock
the deadbolt, your swinging suitcase pushing through
the door before your feet.

a baby who plays with plastic gavels instead of teething keys.
That he knows faces now and that he wants to push out
sounds like words, but can't quite yet. That you talk for him.
That you tell strangers in grocery stores about him.

What I Wanted

The first time, we thought it was a hiccup
in the electricity, a blip in broadcasting,
a balloon tail caught in a tower's steel arms
that crossed invisible waves on a Saturday morning.

The second time, we didn't know what to think,
looked to each other's mouths while the sound
got louder and louder and even at its loudest,
we didn't cover our ears. We listened for some reason.

Months after the TV, the bedroom door locked
on its own accord. You came to the door late,
broke in, grabbed my sleeping wrists, Why would you
lock me out of our room? Where's the key?

Later, I was told that there wasn't a captive tail.
There wasn't a volta, no clever plot that turned on
itself over and over again, just a wife who wanted out,
who wanted free and who waited for the death.

Publication Credits

Where Wedding Bands Go – first published in *Dash*

Your Death – first published in *caesura*

Wreck – first published in *Slant*

Pushing Past – first published in *The Binnacle*

Full Circle – First published in *Boxcar Poetry Review*

They will name you – first published in *ouroboros review*

What You Wanted – first published in *Literary Mama*

What I Wanted – first published in *caesura*

(Some of the poems herein appear in slightly altered forms from the originals.)

Rebecca Cook

Rebecca Cook writes poetry and prose and has published in many literary journals including *New England Review, Northwest Review, New Orleans Review, Wicked Alice, Midwest Quarterly, Story South*, and *Quarter After Eight*. A two-time Pushcart nominee, she was awarded a writer's residency at Dairy Hollow Writers' Colony in 2005, and she was a Margaret Bridgman Scholar in fiction at the 2009 Bread Loaf Writers' Conference. Her chapbook of poems, *The Terrible Baby*, is available from Dancing Girl Press. She teaches creative writing and literature at the University of Tennessee Chattanooga.

Just Another Mary Jane Joke

When Mary Jane had the baby at the mall
she left the little
slimy red thing on the bathroom floor
asleep in the hasty nest of
her Old Navy sweatshirt.

She had seen the tiny turtles
struggling across the beach
the squirmy lizards cracking
out of their shells.

She washed herself
checked her reflection
smoothed her hair
and returned to the movie.

She knew she was a reptile.

Dismembering Flight

I remember heaven's petty jealousies over seating arrangements,
the babble of bickering angels filling the endless days.

I sneaked out in late afternoon, then the sudden sound of gulls screech-
ing as
they reached for me, ganglia-fingers scratching the sky as I flew away.

Now I am shredding these useless appendages, pulling the bones from the
cage
of my ribs, plucking the feathers out.

Their bloody tips are good for writing in, fleshy letters to send toward
heaven,
that universe of eyes watching me still.

Tomato Fish

The tomato-fish moves its fins through seeds,
threads pulp-filled sloughs, veined currents pulling
its spliced gills open and closed in greenhouse air.
Tomato-fish are red, sometimes green, sometimes
fried in southern restaurants where customers feel
them leap up their tongues on waves of red streams
following the motion of their mouths up and down
spoken notes, red fish flowing into vines at the backdoor
where she watches tomatoes treading invisible water—
migrant acrobats moored against the yard.

So Wide

I wish I could swallow myself
When I was little I thought
my father would swallow me,
his mouth so wide I fell into it
every time he spoke.

Curled like a snail in his belly,
my breath a hiccup on his tongue,
I moved small inches into his throat,
careful not to choke him with my tail.
My shell filled up with his juices,
so full on my back, weighing me down
like the house we lived in,
white doors opening in the night.

Curved into my bed, my jaws so wide
my arms fit in. My body folded
back on itself like a sack.
My nipples slipped past my tongue.
I swallowed down my hairless mound,
my thighs, my feet,
the neat package of my toes.

An ugly taste in my mouth wanted water,
a drink from the dark bathroom
down the hall.
I lifted my swallowed self
onto the snail's back and was carried
to the light.

I drank the tepid tap water
under the powder blue ceiling,
the naked bulb hanging over my head.
A limp snake with a full throat.

Snips and Snails

He can't help it.
That wild stuff he breathes.
His heart a hammering fist.
A delighted rage wakes him
in the morning, a powerful joy
lifts him from the pillow.
His dark dream recedes
behind the day.

At breakfast his wiry body is poised
to strike at his cereal bowl.
He jumps. He screams.
His mother sets him in the chair.
He wriggles and squirms
and looks over his shoulder.
In another world he would be

running fast, a mad scent in his nose,
his stomach yearning for a warm throat,
hands ready to rip and taste blood, blood, blood.
In Spring,
when the flowers spread their sex on the air,
he would run with the wild boys,
humping in a frenzied play,
tiny phalluses filling up and throbbing like bees
swarming against each other,
butting and bawling the horrible horny song of maleness
and we wonder what's

wrong and why he isn't content to read his Lucky Charm's
box and trot off to school,
the rules wrapped round his muscle.
Clothed in restraining wires,
a pleasant fence.
His energy ripples, pushes against the structure

and unless he figures it out in time,
realizes that the hunt is over
and everything is *free and easy*,
he'll struggle his way behind
the high barbed wire and bruise his head on walls.
Open his veins in a quiet dance.
Bare his teeth in agony.

Stones

I can't hear what the stone is saying to me,
it speaks too softly. I sit with my face down
because I am ashamed. The rock knows the
grass and the sky and the light on the water,
the shape of my head leaning against the tree.
I am too large to be silent. Too hard to be
listening to hear things, like water falling over stones.

What Despair?

What despair? A flock of starlings might have the same effect
flying straight through the body, splintering the available light.
But the light had gone out. That's what she tried to tell us. How many
ways are there not to listen? She held two stars in her hand, one for her,
one for her daughter. Two points of light. Curled into each other they
were like shells on the bed. Beside them the flames leaped up, the smoke's
gentle arms reached
for them. But it didn't end in the fire. They were saved.
Now the days are tucked into her mouth like stones. Now
the birds come every morning to peck out her soul. They leave just
enough so she remembers everything, every time the sun rises. That shift
of wings moving through her, beating her heart into threads. She's so red
she glows at midnight. She's so broken
her parts rattle like bones in her bed.

Interview With the Soul

Inside marble's cold dream,
I lived a life without breath.
In a temple with strange incense,
in a goddess with no heart.

I lived a child with no brain,
no thought waiting in a silent house.
I slept in a fleshy sleeve while
the body rocked me in its soft ocean.

Many times I was torn from the wall
of the womb before burrowing deep in a willing mother.
I can tell you the taste of breasts and fingers.
My own chapped lips over the clouds of Wednesdays.

In the poet's wrestling belly I heaved and ached,
awash on emotion and unquenching joy.
I watched between breaths while my blood
poured out on a checkered floor.

I'll tell you the only secret I know.
I'll whisper it and you can hear it next week
when the shrink-wrap falls from your hands.
When the truth opens your throat against the sand,
and your ears uncoil from dreaming.

Listen.

Dressing the Discarded Shadow

I dreamed I took your cancer into
my body and healed us both–
ate your mottled liver,
knotted lymph and crackling bone.
Swallowed your blood and peppered fluids
before I buttoned your abandoned skin onto mine,
snapped your empty knuckles tight
to my fingers and waited for us to breathe,
for our grafted lungs to gather the stale air.

But when I see you, I am disappointed.
The pain I keep expecting–
the million, chewing mouths slowly
savoring your insides–seems never to start.
I am cheated.

Unable to follow the inevitable arc of your death,
to be glad when you touch my face
like a mother should when her days are numbered,
when the distance between us has hardened
like drifted wood, porous enough to let the pain flow through,
I stiffen before your smile, lace my fingers together
in a net to catch whatever might break loose–
whatever might slip past and pull me under.

Clickity Clack

Concerned about her head full of beetles,
the disease with its three cornered hat ushers the insects
past the gallery of her eyes, turned away from the walls,
away from the streets, fog misting a trail through the city.

The doctors follow, death on one hand, hope on the other.
When they arrive, they open their caskets and doves fly out.
It's all for the best they tell her. She curves her mouth around
the stillborn baby, its tongue smooth as her thoughts, its legs

almost kicking until it remembers it's dead. They unhook
the ceiling so she can stretch a little, both arms unfurling and
billowing before she remembers they're not hers and they float away,
hands waving goodbye, thumbs up and ready, riding
a wave of blue.

The disease speaks in loud bangs, its mouth full of
gunpowder against her face. *Talk to us, talk to us* it says.
The baby stirs up her throat, booted feet digging out her
voice, raw as water, raw as her peeled brain rattling with claws,

golden pinchers snapping the wires holding her up till
she falls through the room, white cotton wings
fluttering the walls as she buzzes past her head full of legs
rasping out words flying from the disease's full, full mouth.

Love Poem

This bed is heavy with me and the weight of you pressing deep inside,
while the stillness listens to the small, sharp sounds we make. The air
reaches to touch the warmest parts of me with its cool hands, its caress
on your hands on my shoulders, your mouth on my breasts, the sheets in
my fists and the smell of you around me and in me.

Together and alone, floating in an empty space
that spins us down like the drench of rain,
like the bottom falling out of the thing that hits
the earth and flies apart, taking your breath just before you reach the
surface. Before you wake from the dream and know
you'll remember.

I am rising up from the bed and watching us
from all the corners of the room.
Everywhere at once, wrapped around you,
laughing and breathing in the thing that is you and me,
hidden behind the covers,
asleep in the dark and heavy sounds of our breathing.

Publication Credits

Just Another Mary Jane Joke – first published in *Wicked Alice*, Winter 2003

So Wide – first published in the poem trio "Father in Three" in *Mad Hatter Review* 2005; second printing in the chapbook *The Terrible Baby*, Dancing Girl Press, March 2006.

Dressing the Discarded Shadow – first published in *Tar Wolf Review*, Summer/Fall 2005; second printing in the chapbook, *The Terrible Baby*, Dancing Girl Press, March 2006.

Ray Zimmerman

Ray is a former president of the Chattanooga Writers Guild and won Second Place in the 2007 poetry contest of the Tennessee Writers Alliance. He read his winning poem, "Glen Falls Trail," at the awards ceremony of the Southern Festival of Books at Legislative Plaza, Nashville, Tennessee, ten days after undergoing coronary bypass surgery. His chapbook, Searching for Cranes, received favorable commentary in Bloomsbury Review. He has organized poetry readings at Pasha Coffee House and other Chattanooga venues. Ray was the subject of a feature article in the September 2008 issue of Blush magazine.

Dance

When Sally walked a mile and a half
to the neighbor's barn dance
she didn't think of the walk back.

She danced with every boy that asked,
encouraged a few that didn't.
Too young to be serious, she just craved fun.

No cars passed on the highway.
Gas was scarce
in 1933.

Darkness covered the land;
only a crescent moon
lighted her path.

Bob offered to walk her home;
she welcomed company, even
when he suggested the short cut.

Passing the old cemetery, she asked
"Do you think they know we are here?
Do you think they mind our presence?"

"Whichever one of us dies first
will have to come back
and let the other know."

"We won't even know who's here."
"Oh yes we will, the one that comes back
will dance a jig to let the other know."

She had forgotten their encounter
when the storm came that winter
and wind howled through the house.

Floorboards of the attic rattled,
the tapping got louder.
Her sisters cried in alarm.

Her daddy took his gun and said,
"You stay here while I have a look."
He returned with no shot fired.

"There is nothing up there," he said,
his face twisted to strangeness.
He wouldn't let the others go see.

Sally heard Bob died that night,
thought of how the noise sounded
like someone dancing a jig.

Sign

Mercury:
element
metal
liquid
toxic.

Tennessee River waters contain
Mercury,
not the space capsule,
but the element,
metal
liquid
toxic.

Tennessee River fish contain
Mercury,
not the space capsule,
but the element,
metal
liquid
toxic.

Pregnant women
should not eat
these fish.

Nursing mothers
should not eat
these fish.

Children
should not eat
these fish.

Adult males
may eat
these fish.

Women past childbearing age
may eat
these fish.

Elderly people
are encouraged to eat
these fish.

Homeless people
are required to eat
these fish.

That's all.
Have a nice day.

Cranes

Their voices
call to my ears,
pull my eyes skyward,
heard before sighted,
Sandhills from Michigan.

Cranes overhead
wing southward,
call my thoughts to fly with them
to Okefenokee
or the Gulf Coast of Florida.

The cranes arrive,
bring their news of winter,
their voice compared to barking
geese, to the bugling
of wild elks.

These are no geese,
their words no honk,
no barnyard bark for them.
It is a rattling coo,
doves amplified 1000 times.

Arrows shot from a bow,
they neither swoop nor slow,
they rocket southward,
abandon me here
rooted to the ground.

Glen Falls Trail

I climb the limestone stairs
through an arch in rock,
into the earth's womb,
pass through to a surprise:

George loves Lisa painted on a wall.
I wonder, did he ever tell her?
Did she ever know or think of him,
raise a brood of screaming children?
Did they kiss near wild ginger
above the stony apse?

Did lady's slipper orchids
adorn their meeting place
where deer drink from rocky cisterns?
Did their love wither
like maidenhair fern,
delicate as English Lace?

The symbols have outlived the moment.
There is only today, only
the murmur of water underground,
my finding one trickle into a pool.

I never knew this George or Lisa.
The rock bears their names in silence,
names the stream forgot long ago.

Reincarnation

An old black vulture landed in a tree
overlooking Chickamauga Creek;
gave me a sidelong glance.

I thought of Edward Abbey,
critic of government agencies,
professor and park ranger.

Abbey is buried in an illegal grave;
a cairn of stones covers
his remains.

His friends saw to his request,
wrote on one stone,
"Edward Abbey, no comment."

The nemesis of Glen Canyon Dam
desired no memorial,
got one anyway.

He always said he'd come back
as a vulture next time,
just seemed fitting.

I looked up into the oak,
said, "Hey there Ed,
looks like a good day for flying."

Abbey didn't say a word
just gave me that sidelong look,
the old buzzard.

Ray Zimmerman

No Hair

No hair
shaved bare,
spread my ribs
from here to there.

Above the table
I seem to float,
cut open like
a sacrificial goat,
a breathing tube
shoved down my throat.

With any luck
alive I'll be.
Catheter in case
I have to pee.
Hope I can pay
this doctors' fee.

Health care
cash cow,
new prescriptions
pay how?
Everyone wants
my money now.

It doesn't matter
when I revive,
I'm simply glad
to be alive.

Dog Star–Isis

Sirius greeted
the crescent moon last night,
followed his master Orion,
bright belt draped across the sky.

The bull fled Orion's sword.
Seven sisters
shunned his embrace.

Cold nights follow warm days.
Already the forsythia blooms,
heart fills with promise of spring.

Dog days of summer far away.
When Sirius rises with the sun,
the Nile floods.

Moonscape

Full moon obliterates
all but brightest stars,
casts shadows on
urban monoliths,
home to rats and divas.

Neon stars announce
coming events.
Rainbows form and dissolve
cold beer, sandwiches,
spicy bikini bar.

Alleys clog with dust.
Grit polishes glass.
I shade my eyes
against smoke and soot.
Wind shakes neon signs.

Full moon rules
above skyline.
Despite burning questions
on combustion,
downtown is looking up.

Ray Zimmerman

Christmas Papers

I was older when I noticed
the same color and pattern
on the Christmas paper.
Each year a pattern
graced a smaller package.

Christmas morning emanated
excitement and opening
packages with scissors,
carefully cutting tape,
so as not to rip the paper.

I was older when I noticed
my mother's hands,
ironing on Christmas night.
She ironed the same towel
again and again.

Under the towel
Christmas papers
lost their creases,
regained smooth surfaces.

Her hands rolled the paper
we could not replace. Choosing
between gifts and new paper,
she chose gifts.

Ray Zimmerman

Snow

Already the snow dissolves
at seven in the morning
in the Chattanooga dawn.

It returns me to an Ohio childhood.
I drag my sled uphill
to skid back down again.

I conclude the days sledding,
await my dad's return,
a rabbit in his hunting coat.

Blood and guts defile
the whitest landscape,
cleaned up by dogs.

My mother, busy in the kitchen
with rabbit in a pan,
vegetables from a Mason jar.

Birdshot lead between my teeth,
I cannot taste the flesh
washed down with milk.

Awakened from this dream,
I breakfast on oatmeal with raisins,
snow already melting.

Moonbeam

Flame-red hair,
dressed in black,
surfing down a moonbeam
she dances under oaks.

Bare feet on mossy turf,
gathering shed skins of snakes,
she buries a dog skull
'neath tobacco and herbs.

Pale skin in bare moonlight,
on a mountain top
she presses next to me.
Full moon burns through a tree.

Screech Owl

Home from hospital
I heard
the owl call back
his great-horned kin
hooting and blustering
outside my window
all through the night
my mother died.

He came back to announce
my father descending
into a coma.

I sought the sound
of my name
in his voice.

I heard no name
and so I knew
someone else's time
had come, not mine.

Sing your dirge, little owl,
strut before your mate,
harvest a mouse.

Another day you
will call me.
I will be the prey.

Beneath Wild Azaleas

Sprouted on the thinnest soil,
rooted to a rock.
Footholds in fissures,
dappled sunlight
scattered on your leaves
nourishes root and branch.

Icy water numbing toes
above a waterfall,
I cling to rock
upon the cliff.
Water cascades to the abyss.

Only you and I see
the girl with golden hair,
haloed by the sun,
one hand in mine.

She drops your July flowers,
white as her pale skin,
to float on mountain waters,
a message to the land below.

Childhood's Twilight

In those days the devil's workshop
occupied our basement.
First floor rooms were dirty storefronts
on the verge of bankruptcy.
Small apartments nestled on upper floors,
ours the first door on the right.

Families sought scant refuge here,
town drunks and whores thrown in
to emphasize the misery.
The days, iron gray
with clouds to hide winter sun.

Phantoms of past days creep
like shadows from beneath
a rusty railroad bridge at 4 AM.

I return to the sulfurous smell of burning coal.
Radiators rattle, engorged with steam.
I awake, the pipes expand with
a clang, clang, clang of steam and heat.
Another steam releases moaning in the rooms above.

It is not Vulcan at his forge I hear,
it is not Thor defending Valhalla.
The devil's hammer clangs and clangs and clangs,
forging iron cages for the souls he captures.
His goat-hoofed feet dance on concrete
in the fiery glare.

Publication Credits

Sign – first published in *The Pittsburgh Quarterly, TPQ Online*

Cranes – first published in the *Chattanooga Chat*, newsletter of the Chattanooga Chapter of the Tennessee Ornithological Society.

Glen Falls Trail – won second place in the Tennessee Writers Alliance 2007 poetry contest. Ray read the poem at their awards ceremony at Legislative Plaza, Nashville, Tennessee, at the Southern Festival of Books. "Glen Falls Trail" was subsequently published by www.vinestreetpress.com.

Reincarnation – previously published in the *Earth First! Journal* under the pseudonym "Mockingbird."

Sign, No Hair, Moonscape, and **Dog Star–Isis** – published in *Presenting the Beatniks*, an anthology of works read at the Second Beatnik Poetry Reading of the Trenton Arts Council (Trenton, Georgia)

Moonscape – first published on the window of the CreateHere gallery in Chattanooga during an exhibit of environmental art.

Ray read **"No Hair"** and **"Sign"** in the third Beatnik Poetry Reading of the Trenton Arts Council and appears in the DVD production of this performance accompanied by The Drum Circle, with interpretive dance by the Contrapasso Dance Company.

E. Smith Gilbert

E. Smith Gilbert is a pseudonym. The writer is a native of Atlanta. He is a retired businessman. He has been published in the United States and Great Britain. He is currently involved in documentary film. He is a former member of the Chattanooga Writers Guild Board of Directors.

The Marked Sojourner

Twice driven out, expelled,
I passed through the tunnel to all worlds
Through the Gate to other lands.
I could not turn back because of steel and fire.
The face of that angel was livid with murder.
A forest of hands raised against me.
I'd had the best of all mothers, the first of them all.
She was ever curious and angry
Because of what she thought was denied her.
I journeyed East, seeking a livelihood and water
Where in some visible paleness of forgetful light,
Out of much desert, there might be green land to hold fast.
In spite of my scar, the illumination of my skin,
I saw many things and tasted much of bitter and sweet fruit.

E. Smith Gilbert

Old Preachers and Weakness
in Water Drops

Old preachers knew it.
They'd tell it,
Rant against it,
They knew it, real well.
It was as always,
Its triangle head carrying stinging fire
And thick fat coils hidden just beneath the creek bank
Possible even at baptisms
No matter how close to home cool saving waters flowed
It'd burn…
Burn… *Lord*… *Gawdalmighty…the heat of it all*
Children, it burns… burn…burning hell fire!
In spite of Righteousness…it's coiled there…
Unseen until far, far too late.
Known by prophets
As old as the gates of the beginnings
Of the gates of the world
With the placing of the sun and the moon…
Those man-blood-envy eyes
In that arrow-point shaped head
Reflecting back cold moonlight,
Holding enough poison to boil away all moisture in all flesh.

E. Smith Gilbert

Dreams on the Blade of a Dagger Reflected in Bright Sun

He took the boy, fuel, and some water,
All that might be needed;
They headed toward barren territory.
He took the truth of it all,
The emptiness of the land into his eyes
With the sun running on the keen iron he lifted.
His heart was cut by the demand
Perhaps as his sweating hand
Tightened on the smooth polished horn knife handle.
He needed brutal, fast strength to make his kill
And not be distracted by a blameless voice.
He thought of a dead man abandoned in the desert, left to burn
Just before thousands of years of dreams, desire, and prophecy Fell on
him.

Clinic

Once, I worked in a mental health clinic.
The halted, broken, addicted,
those gone missing
Into unreadable dreams
Came for futile blessing,
the only attention they'd ever had.
The place was a false Lourdes
with failing rituals of lack:
Talk, lectures, warnings, piss tests, shots, increasing medication.
Their faces of any color, indistinct, all pale.
Most of them were humped from carrying
Something gray you could never see.
I saw a woman there with matted sauerkraut hair;
She shook and rocked side to side.
The file said she was in her early forties –
She looked a damn rough ninety.
She was dried up, had broken breasts, a failed gut,
Had screaming eyes that were loud.
She told me, "My life as I knew it is over...
I knew it would happen...
All I do is wait until sleep."
I couldn't and didn't do a thing.
Sometimes what there is, is,
and all there is, is night.

E. Smith Gilbert

A Fatal House Fire in Rural North Georgia

With the suddenness of all burning houses,
It surprised them all that winter,
This growing lethal star
Stepping out from night.
A heat without mercy, long living
In the old man's by then cooling heart.

Their old mother had long ago left the stubbornness of men.
She fled the fire to the empty dirt yard,
Holding in her eyes children
lost to her forever.

The boys ran deep inside their father's house,
But he was beyond their reach
In his house with its core of flammable resinous pine heart
That had stood for years
Close to a plot of small graves
With small stone peg markings,
Injuries of time:
Family dead of age, accident, failure, stillbirths.

The old man, ever stubborn,
Refused to leave the exploded kerosene star fire
Eating the kitchen.
When the spine of the house crumpled,
He still thought he could break, scatter and bury it all.

E. Smith Gilbert

Mid-morning, what remained was found:
Burned out stove,
Charred hand-pieced quilts,
Brittle dust ghosts of photographs,
The fire-melted steel double barrels of a shotgun.

The weeping of women cannot ease
The bursting fermented hearts of old men;
Sons are seldom able to rescue their fathers.

E. Smith Gilbert

The Old City, Snow in Jerusalem

I remember Jerusalem as a dream of perfect light.
In cold smoky air, in a grey wind,
On my lips, the fluid taste of sleet, then snow,
Then new night on my face.
Now, over coffee, in June,
Sitting in the Diaspora in summer, reading newspapers,
The bite of coffee recalls a January
When snow settled soft over stone,
Wet wind in the *shouk*,
Almonds,
Hazelnuts,
Charcoal fires,
Tobacco,
Bread.
Fast walking,
Rush-push,
Wet crowds passing
Over snow-slicked stones.
A strong scent of bitter coffee,
Passing quick as steam
lifted up in cold wind
as rich as oranges

E. Smith Gilbert

All the Dead have Gone to Nashville

All the dead have gone to Nashville,
Runaway and residing there, stalking,
Then melting into cement sidewalks,
Having tired from staring at
And accosting certain passersby.

Just last Halloween, standing shoulder to shoulder,
God, Death, and the Devil seen on Second Avenue
Accosting each other about mutual assistance agreements,
long-time working arrangements,
problematic deafness,
And congestion on crowded cement sidewalks.

The Three were holding hands;
Each one affectionately kissed the other.
They dressed alike, as they should,
close to being triplets.
It could be seen that one is blind,
Two are deaf, and only the Devil sees clearly,
speaking in a voice as sound as a church bell.

E. Smith Gilbert

The Gospel of Judas

I thought much of Him;
We were as if torn from out of the body of each other.
After the garden
After the hill
When the last of our words fell, spilled
Tumbling down
Scattered on the ground like straw or salt
The efforts of our dealings
were settled, in those fields, on trees.

E. Smith Gilbert

Crows Pillaging Scuppermongs in October

The afternoon we went out the air had cooled
In those fatal last brilliant days in early October,
Waiting for the hard step of frost.
We visited a vineyard,
heavy fruit left pulling down vines.
Lazy pickers had gone to other harvests;
About half the fruit, bright-sun spoiled, half withered,
Fermented into capsules of sugary sharp wine.
We gorged ourselves on wet sweetness,
Standing beneath those breast-heavy arbors.
In chill shade as the sun dulled,
We held in our hands what light there was
While above, crows soared, landed, devoured, and screamed,
Hard pushing each other aside to seize
What they could by force
Beyond any reasonable appetite,
Then flying away at sundown in loud drunken fury,
Lifting their coarse net.

E. Smith Gilbert

In Chicago

The year we divorced,
When we had already separated,
We danced together at that fancy formal wedding,
The one where I was best man,
Where the special yarmulkes were pastel-colored silk.
Rare lush flowers were on every table
In the big old hotel.
Where the ballroom windows overlooked the city,
You could see where some things came close to sky.
The song we danced was your favorite;
I drank a lot of champagne
In some far-flung, maybe frail, hope
and asked you to my room.
You emphatically declined.
That night, and before my plane the next day,
I slept with a friend of the bride.
I can barely recall the wedding,
But it was late in winter.
Cold grey, the sky spit snow that morning.
I remember and know dreams dissolve;
Dances can't be saved.

In the Jewish Cemetery

That late afternoon, clouds were the lead grey of a watercolor.
The Holidays done, we were in that seasonal stop
between early autumn and winter.
We were watching the weather as much as seeing graves.
We made the obligatory petitions over the graves
And cleared a small measure of overreaching grass
Away from the face of the still polished stone of your dead lover.
I made sure you left a few small stones,
Calling cards used with the dead.
Pebbles, small evidences of recollection.
We walked around a new-filled grave,
The heavy clay fill, responding to recent rain, had started to sink.
I remembered that funeral had been a couple of days ago;
You became hurried to leave.
You, concerned about the cold pin-fine rain beginning to fall.

E. Smith Gilbert

What Is Left Inside Old Houses

On sunny days
Recollecting days of rain,
I think of wet ground darkening by water,
Blackening with rainfall,
Thick thighs spread
Clasping water.

Of old houses on small lots, magic.
Knowing naked couples once locked there,
Windows raised inside,
A visible track of sunlit dust
Some residual blood spore.
Common in crime, those ghosts of our dead lovers,
Ever present, with the movement of our breath.

E. Smith Gilbert

Collecting in the Ruins

When the new public park beside the river was built,
Old, years-empty buildings were knocked down.
Where the bulldozers cut,
Many things hidden became visible.
A hundred years ago
This place had been a riverboat port.
Here there had been warehouses,
A pharmacy,
Coal dealer,
Barroom.
In the cut made by the dozers,
Sunlight struck muddy resurrecting glass,
Colored glass
Clear,
Green,
Brown,
Buried then resurrected
With a broken knife
With cracked bone handles,
Whiskey bottles,
Medicine flasks,
Coins – some a hundred years old,
Copper and silver stained by corrosion,

One gold coin found in loose ground
Among some brass and horn buttons.
You collected all these as fast as a beggar
Gathering found windblown wealth.
You spoke of these finds as a kind of mail.
In the wind that came up toward sundown,
I watched your hair move.
Each wind-burst in your night-black hair danced
Thick as feathers on the back of a night-dark bird.

You spoke how the coming rain
Would expose more relics, treasure to you.
At dusk you found an unbroken bottle,
A brown medicine jar,
Near a crushed rusted watch
Buried alongside a rust-paralyzed pistol
Next to a still full half-pint of cheap, clear whiskey.
All of these you collected in your sack
With the other glass and the half-bladed knife.
By the time we got home,
October rain was hitting fast and hard.
You washed your treasures in my kitchen sink,
Dried them, disinfected the sink,
Wrapped your treasure,
Labeled each piece with the date found,
Like a postmark.
That night we lay naked,
Kissing in our bed, hearing hard rain.
In thirty days, the lot on the river side
Was paved over
And you had left.

Catch in Midair

At the end of autumn
On one of the bright sun-days before frost
The wind gained speed.

One afternoon we walked through a garden of tall dahlias.
Bold with their laughing colors,
Fat, baroque, flowers defied soon-coming frost.

On that afternoon
You held a bunch of just-cut blossoms;
Intense yellows, reds, whites vibrated in my eyes.

You standing among the flowers
Were brightly balanced between colors and strong white sun.
Standing in smiles as if you had just been caught flying.

E. Smith Gilbert

Figs and Pears

At table, in early winter,
Eating preserves on thick toast
Spread with a silver knife
Twin in color to cold deep afternoon sky:
Dark figs and sweet pears,
Sweet heavy flesh, sun-ghosts, sugar mummies.

At table, meals in midwinter dark,
Those bright jars, bottles of small suns,
No matter how slight
Keep what we can hold in hand
Savor in mouth
Push against the barren into warmer days.

Being Bathed in the Polio Hospital, 1951

They bathed us.
As I remember,
It was frequent.
But I was a child, long ago.
It was they said, therapy,
But such might be also, for some, chance sin-cleansing.
The heated water was a blasting Babel,
Speech in foreign tongues
Screamed sermons bubbling like a false Jordon.
Steam against withered legs.
They bathed us like a riptide,
Secured tight on rough canvas in tubs.
Steam bounced
In the heat-heavy, white room.
On white tile walls, it made thick dew
While my death-pale soft legs strove against corpse-grey canvas
Laced tight, cord looped like tent ropes of sojourner's camps,
Tight through brass grommets discolored green by hot waters.
Water rose and pooled against skin and seized the heated bones.
Who was I, so small and expelled from home,
To strive against stronger hands,
When screaming on my white days in the white tile room.

Helga Kidder

Helga Kidder received a BA in English from the University of Tennessee and an MFA in Writing from Vermont College. She is a co-founder of the Chattanooga Writers Guild and leads their poetry group. Her poetry and translations have been published in many journals and anthologies. Her translation chapbook Gravel was published by Poetry Miscellany Chapbooks, UTC, Chattanooga, in 1994. Her chapbook *Why I Reach for the Stars* was a finalist in the Firewheel Chapbook competition.

Another Season

The moon's final blush fades in my early waking,
in cinnamon plums painted on the cup
between my hands. I sip coffee, watch dawn
fan open the sky, taste again German summers,
those ground-fog mornings Mother and I
picked plums. And like a Bible story, she'd tell
of my birth on August 9, at the height of plum season,
how she awakened to dawn plucking her ripened fruit,
how she muttered her way to the town hospital:
too many plums, she thought, too many. Plums,
she'd insist, signify change, as when the moon's
brown ring portends a season concluding.
Bitter first, then sweet is memory's taste,
these brushed plums on my cup.

Helga Kidder

O'Keeffe's *Purple Petunia*

Look at the face of this bloom.
Night in her darkest finery.
Those shadowy eyes.
Such hollows
preserve memory:

Mother's last request:
I rubbed her soles with spirits
so she could slip
away
quieter than a pocket door.

Forced
through another passage,
another birth,
in darkness
light knocked at my throat.

Book of Nature
- for Lauren

Just once I dress-rehearsed shedding my skin
like a serpent in mother's *Buch der Natur*

locked in the *vitrine*. I remember my eighth
grade hikes through other bound works,

how mother's brows purled after Frau Vogt
said between hinges and door how beautifully

heels shaped my legs. Mother's solution
slipped me into Mary Janes, lowered

my expectations. That fall, between my
moon face & grades, my career adviser

shook his head, studied my hands & fingers,
their lengths, as if they were tools.

Without raising his voice he advised, next year
I should begin my apprenticeship with the town's

midwife. Suddenly seen as handler of intimacy
between husband & wife, I blushed, pleaded

with the sun's rays in the window to bury
my skin in red fallen leaves.

So when you insisted today, *Grown-ups
don't know everything*, I remembered recess,

others' giggles & fingers pointing at mine.
To my surprise & yours, I agreed.

Helga Kidder

Landscape

I
The piano keys winked black & white
I didn't understand standing
dumb in grandmother's room
dependent on mother's hand
that would lead me
for fifteen more years
until I took another's.

II
His words played ring around
the rosy behind my eyes,
paused, began again confused,
could not keep London Bridge
from falling down
into a pit
of ashes, ashes
this side of eternal life,
a lonesome offing
for a woman
such as I.

III
In the last train entering the decade,
memory is a passenger
fidgeting in the sameness of scenery,
pastoral in its theme,
its sentiment sad & good & holy:
A melancholy of inevitable arrival.

Sky mottled blue is birdsong,
moon a hand at night.
In between
I find myself
over & over.

Discourse of Pleasure

(Tula Telfair's oil on canvas)

Gorged clouds suspend dawn's first blue
above fields still dreaming
in night's shadow.
      Land will awaken soon,
stretch its limbs through inlets
to the mouth of the sea.
        Then earth's tongue
will speak to moored water, arid mounds,
of coming release.

Helga Kidder

Coming of Age

Tyger, tyger burning bright
in the forests of the night . . .
                    William Blake

When wishes have birthdays,
my good hand worries
the page like a tiger pacing
the length of his cage.
The windows stare
silent on winter woods.

I need all of tonight:
Summer straddling the kitchen sill,
his arms around me curdling
milk in the saltware pitcher,
my right hand listening
to the pace of his heart.

How should I measure
this handful of summer
in winter?

The tiger tries to forget cage
yet listens to the heart,
remembers wild promises:
our future's lissome steps
like stars in this bountiful sky.

Oh night, center me
in your *milky way*, let his words
fade into a black hole
so this tiger calms,
lapping memory's bowl.

Calla Lilies
-for Gerlinde

No doubt, the one below, the one leaning in
is submissive, perhaps kneeling . . .
Then why the need for one more,
a watcher, standing in back, outside
of marriage behind the two who
have lived together too long?
Look at *Three White Lilies*,
a ménage à trois, O'Keeffe's apparent
arrangement of disgrace.
Or is it grace that rains
through all seeds, grace that allows
a way to survive? I used to smile
at the moon's plump face attuned
to a night's symphony, the arrangement
of stars, assured that a triangle's
overt clang, clang was useless
to harmony. I wonder if O'Keeffe knew,
too, a man's coiling, twisting
claims of innocence the way a woman
soon learns to deny the moon's phase
within her. Either way, she straightened
herself like a lily to the sun, half-smiled
at the day, allowed how she might as well
gather grief in her skirt and place it
to rest for the night like a whiney child.
Who's to blame if she's learned to keep
herself bound closely at the chest?

Birthday Cornucopia:
Adonis Blue, Tyler and the rabbit, and sourwood honey

This morning my dog scouted the garden,
its tangle of blackeyed susans and maidengrasses,
for the rabbit he'd pointed out in yesterday's dusk.
His barks blew breath on the sliding glass door.

Yesterday, in a shop window, I saw me as a
dancer fluttering like a garden's *Adonis Blue*
but instead recognized mother's rounded shoulders,
her thick-set middle, her hobbled walk.

The rabbit hopped to the door, nibbled
the green of the doormat at leisure, too young
to know delayed danger until I clapped hands.
He sheered zigzag across sprouting lawn.

Earlier the postman left a Savannah Bee
Company box at the door. Hesitantly, I cut
the tape, unfolded layers of tufted cardboard
to six taster jars of Appalachian honey.

Though the rabbit has not shown again, Tyler
still sits and guards the sliding glass door.
Perhaps the rabbit delved into the woods behind
the house. Perhaps Tyler counts on siblings.

He mostly chases butterflies. Today I tasted honey
like a birthday, complex with a hint of sour. Out front
a canopy of trees compose shade, but rays warm
like sourwood honey: in sweet, small batches.

Helga Kidder

Why One Should Let Sleepers Lie
- for Galen

A tree surgeon & his chipper crew rip-saw
this fine Southern dawn of row houses at an hour
what the hell . . . the neighbor arranged
fed up with branches brushing upstairs
panes at his perfect moment's climax
or in his finality's drift-off to sleep – oh
to think of the morning that might have been:
A starry-eyed stretch & curl-back-up
in the bed, turning over the hour glass
as it sifts flour for our daily bread
next to the dog's cocked ears to dust tracing
the dresser until noon ambles in & sips
Mint Juleps on the rocking chair porch.

Looking out, the tree surgeon, hoisted to bedroom
height in a bucket like a minor god, cuts away
the years, limb by limb, of unchecked behavior
for recycle–the crew feeds the chipper–
a thrust, grind, then a thud.
As if this were not enough, the neighbor's whim
pulls an engine cord, starts mowing the one-row
lawn, then blows leaves & debris
between fire walls, saws one board of pine
into pieces for the lowest of higher purposes
at this ungodly hour, Judgment Day,
what the hell . . . not one of us fast enough
to cover up. Even the dog howls.

Potential

In this age of robots and instant gratification,
thank God, I still sadden at a golf ball-
sized skull discovered gardening,
shudder at an immature serpent
caught in the rake among dried leaves,
easily coaxed between rocks.
After blackberry winter and misting rain
roses repay with profusion—a transition
lifting the mind off the ground, nose
closer to home and potato soup inside.

My Mother's Day bouquet blooms yellow
in a white basket like new age religion,
for a little while. Current TV shows, the wilder
the better, a step backward. As long as we can
stumble or limp or hop on one foot forward:
as long as our eyes see promise on the horizon,
a light ahead. The way the early hominid
found in Kenya, *Orrorin Tugenensis*, must have,
whose hips and upper legs had begun
adapting to walking upright.

Rooms by the Sea
(Edward Hopper)

The artist filled a fourth of canvas with his look
sidewise out the front door. It is open wide
to nothing but the rippled sea. No stairs, no shore
just blue sky and blue water. Is this how
one should feel, isolated? That there is risk outside
without a life jacket, some craft underfoot?

Inside, the open doorway shapes the morning sun
on entry floor and wall. Then the wall stops,
squeezes the eye into another room, its puzzle pieces:
an easy chair arm below a partial picture hanging
on the back wall, the corner and leg of a dresser
opposite. Light throwing shadows.

One's torn between the open door of opportunity,
the fractured life inside, the destiny of any artist.
Donne said it first. *No man is an island*
then or now. Neither is a woman. Least of all.
To spend a life to fit and re-fit the pieces.
Outside, the sea deep and wide, calling.

Succulents

We live in harsh environments,
water scarce.
We shrivel during drought,
drain what is stored in tissues.
We spend ourselves.
We ache. We grieve.

But when we are given freely,
we expand, our stems swell.
We send forth blooms
like the *claretcup*, deep purple,
red as life blood.
Then we come to our own.

Zeitgeist

I will give you a new heart and put a new spirit in you.
                                        Ezek. 36:26

You want to be a New Year every year, naked
as a baby without pretense & pills,
little & blue enough to turn pee sky blue,
enough to take away the bones' ache,
a kind of world suffering Germans call
Weltschmerz. How it turns traitor,
ready to side with every temptation &
surrenders to them all. *Your flesh is not you,*
is not the real you, someone said. You listen.
The reasons? You have two ears, only one
mouth. Every New Year the same ghosts appear
as if they'd been given permission slips
as if you had never changed your mind.
Is it a wonder, the creator blued the sky,
greened the earth, gave you a chance
to whiten your steps from particles
of the world's dust, *Umweltverschmutzung*,
clinging to your life? Doesn't the sun send
light in minutes, the moon in seconds
to brighten in you the creator's image?
How easily ideas revert to ox carts
traveling old ruts, gravity's pull
for reckless hours, the hours of feasting.
What part of you is fallen Eve or Adam?
You crave more *Lebensraum*, more space
you need to live in loved & satisfied.
Excuses line the heart like spiders running
amok inside the self, unable to tear
true self from self, that is, the first flesh.

Publication Credits

Another Season – first published in *The Heartland Review*

O'Keeffe's *Purple Petunia* – Alabama State Poetry Society – 1st Place

Book of Nature, Calla Lilies – first published in *Heart Rhythms –Anthology*

Why One Should Let Sleepers Lie – first published in *Free Focus*

Potential – first published in *The New Verse News*

Rooms by the Sea – first published in *Woman Made Gallery*

Succulents – first published in *Common Ground Review*

Zeitgeist – first published in *Relief: A Quarterly Christian Expression*

K. B. Ballentine

KB Ballentine received her MFA in Poetry from Lesley University, Cambridge, MA. She has participated in writing academies in both America and Britain and holds graduate and undergraduate degrees in English. She currently teaches high school theatre and creative writing, and she is an adjunct professor for a local community college. She has also conducted writing workshops throughout the United States. Published in many print and online journals, KB has two collections of poetry: *Fragments of Light* (2009) and *Gathering Stones* (2008), published by Celtic Cat Publishing. A finalist for the 2006 Joy Harjo Poetry Award and a 2007 finalist for the Ruth Stone Prize in Poetry, KB also received the Dorothy Sargent Rosenberg Memorial Fund Award in 2006 and 2007. KB's Irish heritage has shaped many of her poems and continues to be a source of inspiration.

Canning for Winter

Rough-tongued raspberry skirts
the artless field, filters sun, rain,
the willful moon. Just yesterday
our sons embraced pails full of red
to greet you at noon, bloody juice
smearing shirts, staining hands.
Your nod, lingered phone call revealed all.

Today I listen to you limping
toward another excuse. Steam
spools from boiled jars flickering
in the sun. Kitchen window frames
the stale yard, the broken swing.
I've fooled myself, pretending
you'll fix it, this. Clouds whisk
the blue, your voice dissolves to static.

K. B. Ballentine

Absolution

Gray skies grimace over the ridge.
October's ambers and rubies
have fallen, turned to fragments
little boys scuffle through.

The heavens dark by four, I light
lamps around the house, the only hope
in an expanding night. He drives
home through guilty rain.

Civil War, 1989

I can still see the paneled walls our portrait smiled from –
that farce of family superior to the real business of yelling
and tears in the living room below, carpet blue with confusion.

One day our family was whole, intact; the next, Daddy
walked his suitcase out the front door without looking back
to see me waving goodbye, believing he would come home.

We saw him next – Joe and Florence and me – at the
diner, his arm around a bleach-blonde he introduced
as "My friend, Janie." Her hand on his leg told me all.

Momma disappeared at dawn to waitress, clerk, any kind
of work she could get, three kids and a mortgage on her
sloping shoulders, and re-emerged at dusk to tuck me in.

But Flo rose with Momma to make us breakfast and Joe quit
basketball to cook dinner and school harbored us during the day,
a haven from the empty house where night-time crept too close.

And the picture is in the attic safely stored, sealed in newsprint
where time never changes, while we grew up in that in-between
place that doesn't choose a side, and can't, because the love
and hate are too strong.

Coal, Inc.

My father knew only darkness.
Six of seven days he'd swelter
in the belly of the earth,
enclosed by dirt and rock,
covered with coal dust that soaked
into the skin,
       the soul.
Coal that bled from the inside
             out and stained
the surrounding hills with rust.

At night he rocked
the baby's cradle with blackened
hands and after supper settled
in with sour mash.
            Each morning
I rose to the smell of biscuits baking
on a stove he'd already stoked and fired;
Momma's stained apron fluttered
in her haste to get him out the door before
the whistle blew.

Once, he told me
he imagined the mine's blackness
was shade cast by giant oaks
and every man's lamp a persimmon
waiting to be picked. That's how he made it
till the end of shift, when he'd wind his way
through the jagged maze of rocks
ready to tear a man's hands,
like thorns in a briar patch,
and stagger into the fading sun.

Daybreak at the Old City Park

Eight mallards bathe in the stagnant lake,
nodding, tossing spray over downy backs,
a carnival atmosphere in the dry, still air.
They ignore my trek past their early shower.

Farther along in the wood I linger by a circle
of concrete, filled in and feral with ivy.
A forgotten fountain? Out by the highway
cars hum and a train clatters its tracks.

Caramel-colored pine needles dust the moss,
and I head toward the fading water. Wrinkled
cans, old bottles, even a pair of muddy galoshes
unveiled to the deer nosing their way to the bank.

No clouds again today. No hope of rain.
Gnats swarm the scum that stipples olive
water, and pines lean for a drink. Canada geese
yak, one hisses me from her golden-necked

goslings. Reeds rattle as birds feed, try to nest.
A cloud of swallows ink the gathering blue,
and a woodpecker knocks on an oak overhead.
King of the lake, a heron poses on a log.

He gapes, admires his likeness, then darts
his beak, fracturing the surface.

Foreclosure

Slapping air, a sparrow nulls
the silence. Darkness dissipates,
thrushes of song gouge the pre-dawn
glow, goad me from hard-won sleep.

I segue from dream to thought, not ready
for this day. My Chevy crouches in the drive,
packed. I roll over, glimpse mangled
shadows of boxes bristling the room,

watch the sunrise here one last time.

Summer in Climax

Bees lumber over clover by the river
in the south Georgia heat. No air blows
through the sultry shade as twilight ruins
the all-blue sky, cloudless since noon.
We simmer on the porch, breathless, severe
with words, savoring any puff of breath.

Granny snaps a *Moonshine Kills* hand fan, breathing
currents of quick, warm wind. And the river
trembles under dotted sun and shadow, Sevier
Basin drying, waiting for a squall to blow.
Sapped from their swim in the lake at noon,
the kids sprawl on cotton sheets, ruined

by years of towel duty and plucking rue in
season. Tongues flapped out, the dogs try to breathe,
heads and tails drooped like flowers at noon.
Fireflies swap places with bees by the river,
where a few lively boys try to grab them, blowing
their wings to light the deepening night less severely

than bare bulbs. Porch lights off, no moth wings sever
this summer night. Flies gather around the ruins
of soda and lemonade. In the sluggish air, Sissy blows
damp hair from my face, teasing tendrils with her breath.
Crickets and frogs compete by the river's
edge–a stereo of sound that will be silent by noon.

K. B. Ballentine

Even with drinks and fans, the porch is as warm as noon.
The moon, brilliant and globed, creates sharp shadows, severely
outlining the house. The melody of rocks and river
splashes into night music. No one wants to ruin
the spell with speech, but we step inside to breathe
without mosquitoes, sweating, waiting for the wind to blow.

I dream of shaded skies, storms blowing
the heat east–somewhere far away by noon.
We'll visit on the porch, take damp breaths
of clover and watch the rain tumble in, thrusting severe
currents down drain spouts; we'll laugh at the ruined
wash on the line as clouds renew the river.

Rain runches the river. Abandoned leaves blow,
ruined green jewels shimmering in the pale noon.
A severe gust scoots them downstream, brings us breath.

Frost Line

It doesn't take much, does it,
for the mountain to meet the moon,
flawless globe snagging on jagged
rock. Rising only inches higher
through night, the frosty moon blinks
as dark clouds polish its surface
and dust stars in the November sky.

The night vibrates with a fox's
yap–quail nest betrayed, cratered.
Withered leaves crackle. Feathers
grace the morning light.

Appalachian Pioneers

Passing houses brown with mildew, damp
on a raw March day, the Spitfire chugs
the road, wind snatches my hair. Shadows drop

long and low across the buildings, the bridge.
A town of hope huddled in a cleft between ridges,
Sunbright chased by rivers around the mountain.

Who were the men and women who slashed,
stamped their way through underbrush
to get here—leading horses, hauling furniture

from another life, another world? One more genteel,
more polished; less dangerous, less alive. Why?
Why slop through mud and muck, drag children

through wild brambles, plucking blackberries
in July, hunting grouse in December?
Once here were they trapped—

only peaks ahead and foothills, disappointments
behind? Was this a refusal to fail one last time?
Look at the names they left. Bitter Creek.

Was it the water's taste? Did too many lose
wives and children to disease, crops to flooding?
Rock Creek bounding one side, Black Wolf the other.

Sunbright. A pause between ridges that captured
the light, held it for a moment. Ghosts swarm.

K. B. Ballentine

Awakenings

Kaleidoscopic jolts ended. Silence
chased shuddering brakes, racketing
engine. Steam and smoke bound me,
the ditch gripping my ruined behemoth.

Car door overhead, I pushed the seatbelt
latch, falling like oil from a bottle. The waiting
school children raised me from metal fractures
then left me alone, morning bus claiming them.

My adolescent angels surrendered to its groan
and hiss, merged with faces gaping over open
windows. I limped along the asphalt, each stone,
each dandelion for once distinct. Finches flickered

as trees tugged the sun overhead, and I tried
to remember the last time I listened to their tune.
Swollen buds hung like dew and lawns plumped
green, faded cuttings tunneling the grass.

When had winter shuffled away? I thumped
the door of the nearest house, waking its widow
from forgotten loneliness and memory's kisses,
heard her creaking through the hall, watched

the door open on her withered face.

K. B. Ballentine

Announcing Spring

Little League Cardinals scurry
outfield, and a Norfolk Southern
engine screeches, rattles the dew
damp seats, a transient earthquake
shaking husks that litter the bleachers.

Triple Crown box car wheels squeal
like a thousand nails pitched
onto concrete, clatter the track, eclipse
the bat's whack, our cheers.

We bask in the mounting sun, glasses
glinting like mirrors. Hot dogs, pizza,
peanuts ripple the stands. Graffiti blurs
by, speeding us toward an uncertain
destination. The batter waits.

K. B. Ballentine

Respite

Dew prisms the grass, long pause of night nearly past.
Ridge and mist thwart sun's salute, mute these sacrosanct

moments: porch, swing, coffee. Yellowthroats
warble, stir sleepy rustles from bushes. Sky bruised gray

blossoms into pink, scatters clouds into the blue. Baby mole
limp between her jaws, the neighbor's cat brisks by.

Church bells chime the new hour. I uncurl, ready for the day.

Unnatural Trend

Heat slinks across the streets,
simmers the lake's surface.
Gnats multiply, skim heavy
air, drink its moisture.

Aligned against nature, we emerge
from air-conditioned houses–
spark incendiary motors,
cigarettes. We rush along roads

with no eyes to see sky, trees.
With no ears to hear a quacking mother
meander her ducklings across
our path.

Worn

Work boots on the table, mud
from fields I've never seen. Part
of you still hiding, hidden from me.

Wrinkled leather, time worn
away. In each crease, specks
of farming dust and hay.

Places you've been without me
in open fields of space, gleaning
for tomorrow yesterday's state of grace.

K. B. Ballentine

Publication Credits

Canning for Winter – first published in *Long Story Short*, September 2009

Absolution – first published in *Tipton Poetry Journal*, January 2010

Civil War – first published in *Apocalypse*, 2007

Coal, Inc – first published in *Touchstone: Literary Arts Magazine of Kansas State University*, Spring 2007

Daybreak City Park – first published in *MO: Writings from the River*, 2009

Foreclosure – first published in *Tidal Basin Review*, Spring 2010

Summer in Climax – first published in *MO: Writings from the River*, 2007 (appeared as Climax)

Frost Line – first published in *Bent Pin*, 2009 (appeared as The Dawning)

Announcing Spring and Awakenings – first appeared in *Fragments of Light* published by Celtic Cat Publishing, 2009.

Finn Bille

Finn Bille has been writing, reading, teaching, publishing, and promoting poetry since his teenage years in Copenhagen, Denmark. At Pepperdine College in Los Angeles, he founded the literary magazine *The Expressionist*. At the University of Copenhagen, he contributed to *Polylogue*, a collection of poetry explications and essays (University of Copenhagen Press, 1970). In graduate school at Georgia State University (GSU), he published in the GSU literary magazine and in other Atlanta publications while writing his Ph.D. dissertation on the literary experience, chiefly dealing with poetry.

His article, "The Ultimate Metaphor and the Defeat of Poetry in T.S. Eliot's *Four Quartets*," appeared in *The International Journal of Symbology* in 1972. While teaching summer English courses at the International People's College in Elsinore, Denmark, the college published his chapbook, *Waking Dreams* (1986). While teaching at Baylor School in Chattanooga, Tennessee, he organized visits by poets and sponsored the literary magazine, *Periaktoi*. Bille created and presented poetry workshops at counseling centers and the Art of Living Folk School, 1986-1990. During this period, he also taught poetry-writing courses at Northwest Georgia College. His collection of poems, *Rites of the Earth*, appeared in 1994 with notes on each poem and an article on revision. Bille has published about eighty poems individually in various magazines and anthologies

At the Edge

At the edge of the clearing
at the edge and alone
at the edge of the clearing and alone
I and the deer
at the edge in twilight
and the trees at the edge
bronze sunset light and these trees
alone at the edge
the doe at the edge
the doe in sunset light
the doe stopped and alert
the doe full-eyed and looking askance
the doe at the edge and alone
and I in sunset light
full eyed and direct
at the edge and alone
and the river swift off to the side
and the river's mere glints of light
stab and are gone from the eye's far corner
and the mountain above the river
the mountain there
the trees here
at the edge
the trees reached into the clearing
and the mountain was there
at the edge and alone
and the doe
at the edge and alone
sun mellowed
sun bronzed her flank
at the edge and alone
as she slowly walked
eyes askance and alert

from the edge into the trees
into the deep-shadowed woods
and I
on the edge and alone
saw her there still
her flanks bronzed over
her eyes full and askance
and now in the shade of the woods
I see her there
and I see
on the edge where I stand
the grasses of her feeding here in the edge
not far from the woods
I see the grasses
now catching twilight
now luminous
husks halo dark seeds
grass in full grassness
and here
on the edge and alone
tears come being here and the trees
and the grass and the river
and the doe there and gone
the grass here and more
and I on the edge and alone
and I on the edge of the clearing.

Dane Graves

Stone ships cannot be moved
stone vessels cannot float
stones set in arid hills
can only settle deeper–stay stone
raised by faith in winds
that blow to richer fields
but cannot move the stones
plowed from fertile fields
stone heavy memory of ritual
stone stand against strong winds
that carry lighter vessels out to sea.

Every Time I Hear a Fly Buzz

I am nine years old on Granddad's outhouse seat.
My thighs and hands feel all the touches
that have smoothed the darkened wood.
I have moved the hand-carved latch of oak
to span the gap between pine door and frame
in the circle scribed by our many turnings.

The fly drones on against the dusty screen
like gentle snoring of the sun-still fields
while the secret workings of all our bodies
mingle with the smell of loam and fresh-cut dill.

No matter where I hear the fly buzz, Granddad's
lime-washed, plastered walls surround me
as I sit secure, at ease with all my people
always in sunny summer at the center of the world.

Every Time I Say Goodbye

I see my mother lean
on the brown half door
overhung by thatch of bundled reeds
spotted green and weathered grey.

Her red rag tight around her brow,
she struggles to smile, her knuckles white,
her blue eyes blank as I turn,
my face reduced to memory.

In the Phillips Collection

In Washington, D.C.
In the Phillips Collection,
in a fine frame of gold
–fluted, antique gold–
next to Italian marble
and Chinese cloisonne:
Here hangs Albert Pekham Ryder's
painting of a boat at sea.

The paint shines like the sea,
its white froth flecks
its green-stroked swells
surrounding, enfolding the boat,
its umber-smeared, distended sail,
its rough-stroked, curved
half hidden gunwale
lifts its bow toward clotted paint
of broken clouds
on the far horizon.

The paint has dried wild
as the stormy sea,
captured and mocked
by its golden frame.

Mug

We are alive,
and I have found
my coffee mug:

The tall white one with blue
curved lip, my first-up-
in-the-morning mug
that I would sip at sunrise
in the breakfast nook

that now is gone, dumped
from the tilted kitchen floor
into the wrack below

where I found my mug,
its white glaze shining,
buried in fired, burned
and broken bricks.

My mug survives.
It's only cracked, chipped
and stained with soot.

Nothing but Soil

Nothing left except a sense of the necessity
     for reconstruction
nothing but soil
and a doubt of its own indigenous seed
and a fear
of the limitations of cultivation
     the sumac: scarlet, assertive
the barrenness of produce
     rabbit tobacco like eager velvet
the sterility of fruits
     crabapples and thick-shelled hickory nuts.
My unsoiled hands,
my settled rump,
my idle back
stir
as my steel blade cuts grinding into hope
     cherry trees and rows of corn.

The Old Parson

He waits for stillness among ticking clocks.
Above him, an antique's long hand
quivers, then numbers another minute;
its hour hand points
to the family Bible, surrounded
by embroidered messages of hope
while its shiny disk
oscillates slowly in the dark.

Now time has paused in his cloudy eyes
that no longer follow the pendulum's swing
but turn inward to the rhythms
      of remembered song.
Limp hands on crocheted doilies
reach into seamless eternity,
failing to grasp when required,
the handshakes of time-bound guests.

After mumbled grace and reluctant eating,
he drops a soup-stained napkin
on his way to the study.
Here, books of sermons, concordances,
and commentaries gather dust
around his desk, littered with parts
and tools for repairing clocks.

Finn Bille

He whittles wooden dowels
and caresses the brass while counting cogs.
He polishes a silver pendulum
with a distant, beaming smile,
for he sees himself riding the golden, pendular orb
while another clock-mender tunes the works.
He knows he can hear when the ticking is right,
and he knows this perfection will cause it to cease
when he rides the final, endless swing
that becomes being,
cogless, tickless, and weightless,
mending his time forever.

Portrait

> *Looking as if she were alive; . . .*
> —Robert Browning, "My Last Duchess"

No, it's not a snapshot, but a portrait.
Yes, you were radiant . . . and more, for film
must never hope to reproduce the glow
of preternaturally lucid skin
or cobalt blue of strong-willed innocence
in such a print of black and white, yet here
you are, as seen before the click and as
you came alive and stared with touching trust
developing in darkroom chemicals
from gray to black that had been night-sky blue,
from white to gray that had been sun-touched pink,
from white to brighter strands of golden hair
then fixed and washed to purge all aging tint.
I call that piece a wonder now. Yes, you.

The Puzzle

Animalia-Chordata-Reptilia-Anapsida-Chelonia

My turtle shell carapace plates
did not make it to the replacement list.
They burned and vanished next to the silver coffee urn
we listed with a price.

What price could stick to wonder?
What would it take to buy discovery
in mud of this keratinaceous treasure,
this life design boxed up as nature's puzzle?

Who could re-pay anticipation
of carapace articulation,
of mounting on the wall
this synapomorphy of chelonia,
this icon of consilience?

Silence of Ashes

Silence of ashes

plum wood flute

once blossomed

Starling

When the flames ran up the rafters
they found a way out
through the vent in the peak of the roof.

There, they found the starling,
its beak and flight feathers pressed
into the wire mesh.

The flames licked out the vent
and brightened for a moment
as they devoured bird skin, feathers,
beak and bone.

Finn Bille

Uphill Flowers

All I see are uphill flowers.
For all I know, the downhill's barren
except for blurs and streaks.

Out of the rush and up from the dip,
flowers show like shooting stars
that glow into our heavy air
from vacant space.

I slow down to catch up
with these small worlds
and see this flock of stars
on stalks, of petals stretched
for sun and nodding to my labored breath
as I pedal uphill again.

Finn Bille

Valentine

Raking leaves, I think of you
our many moments
and this one green:
you in the kitchen cutting onions.

Publication Credits

At the Edge – first published in the anthology *Poetic Out*, 2003

Dane Graves – first published in the author's chapbook *Waking Dreams*, Elsinore, Denmark, 1983

Nothing but Soil – first published in *Sahara* Atlanta Poets, 1974

The Old Parson – first published in *The Phone Still Rings by* Etta Pursley Barton, Atlanta, 1989

Uphill Flowers – first published in *Windwatch*, 1984

(Some of the poems herein appear in slightly altered forms from the originals.)

Dan Powers

Dan Powers performed in the acclaimed PBS TV special, *The United States of Poetry*, with Nobel and Pulitzer Prize winners Derek Walcott, Joseph Brodsky, Czeslaw Milosz, and Allen Ginsberg. His poems have been published in *New York Quarterly*, *Wormwood Review*, *Cumberland Poetry Review*, *Pearl*, and other leading publications. He co-edited and appeared in *Something We Can't Name*, an anthology of Nashville's open-mike poetry readings. His first major collection of poems, *Mighty Good Land*, was published by Black Greyhound Media in 2006. Powers hails from Neely's Bend, Tennessee, where, he says, "Men are judged by the size of their tires." An electrical engineer by trade and a farmer by heritage, he retired from the Tennessee Valley Authority in 2002.

Morels

Two years ago, my friend Vantrease
said farming would not pay his bills.
He sold his milk cows and leased
the Sears catalog store in town.
Blackberry vines and sumac
crowd his unkept pasture and the fences sag.
Last week at church, he held out his hands
soft and white for us to see and said,
"A farm is like the strength in a man's hands.
You try hard to keep it, and you lose it."
In the trillium beneath the hickory grove
on our ridge, my son and I find a few morels
and drop them into a brown paper bag.
Our small talk worn thin, we walk back toward the house
through the dew-wet pasture without speaking.
Here, miles from town, without his friends to see,
he reaches across our silent striding
and grasps my hand with all the strength
of his ten years.
Each of us holds on.

Third Missed Payment

I feed the horses, make sure of dry hay.
In the house, my wife moves against the light.
In the den, scattered across the braided rug,
our kids are at their homework
while the TV gives the evening news to no one.
The old windmill erected by my grandfather
whirls its blades against the red edge of the world.
In the dusk of winter, we are surrounded.
At the edge of the woods, darkness unfolds early
to take the fields.

Early Frost

Last month you reminded me
all our friends divorced years ago.
Last night you came home late.
We both pretended sleep.
Today you have followed October's sun
from room to quiet room, not speaking,
wading barefoot and alone
in each small pool of light.
All day you have escaped me,
returning to the windows
for something in the distance.
Beside you at the window,
my hand in the small of your back,
I see below us marigolds
tinged black by early frost,
maple leaves littering the walk.
The woman from the next farm
down the road comes by to say
the coming winter will be hard.
Your hand rises to your lips,
as if to keep yourself from saying
what you have not.

Rain

Four years of drought.
Now we have rain.
Rain too late for last season's crop
keeps this one in the fields.
The new John Deere, not paid for,
sits stiffly rusting in the shed.
Used to be our fathers might lose
one cow each season.
Now it's a farm in every county.
We have forgotten what to say,
so we mumble over cups of coffee
around our kitchen tables
about the ones who haven't quit,
about the reasons not to,
or to go ahead, sell out
before we lose it all.
Outside the church on Sunday,
old men in older ritual
light each other's cigarettes and pipes
and fill the stained-glass air
with words of crops and cattle.
Smoke lifts from their faces,
forever turned to sky and clouds.
We fill our mouths with words
as we try to find a language
for understanding God,
for believing in the miracles
held out above our heads.
The last of my wife's egg money
shimmers above the offering plate,
a small weak candle
burning in her fist.

Good Rabbit Dogs

Shotgun cradled in the crook of his arm,
my father waved from the snow-covered rise.
His canvas hunting jacket bulged with unlucky rabbits.
He turned to whistle the beagles from the field.
With a sharp pocketknife I met him outside the shed.
He handed me the jacket.
While he penned the hounds, I reached in,
withdrew the limp warm cloths of fur.
The bowl of salty water turned red.
For a few minutes, smoking his pipe,
he stood beside me. "Here, like this," he'd say–
grim, but somehow joyful.
We weren't poor people, but he was raised that way
and this was only right.
When I asked about it, he looked across the field,
wiped his hands on his pants and said,
"Every morning the world is created new,"
and he strode into the house to my mother.
Good summers of rain, high grasses,
meant fat rabbits at the edge of winter.
The hounds wailed happiness
every time my father neared their pen.

Powerhouse

Descending into the smoky basement
of the powerhouse, at the railing
above the rows of heavy pumps,
above the roar of horses galloping beneath the earth,
I've come here to find my father, the millwright,
among sweating iron men
who toil in half-lit incandescence,
each one's manifest destiny glistening on his brow–
men who accept relentlessly
their portioned unrelenting sameness,
their banishment from the Garden taken, final,
men who have not turned back
from God's cold passion for revenge.
I stand here above them,
dark shadows curling from their faces.
I stand amazed, see how they drag their bodies
into each slight detail of machinery and labor,
how tomorrow is today and yesterday.
Iron men rusting toward the end,
my father stands tall among them,
somehow a music in his body,
the way he stood on our porch at night
as moon and stars walked up the stream
beyond the wood fence.
To hear him say,
"Great men die in turn, one by one.
The merely good fall en masse."
When I tell him I don't understand,
he doesn't try to make me.

Evidence

My wife and I hold hands
in the little Presbyterian church above the swale
between the highway and the apple hill
among twenty-five others–dresses and overalls,
sweatshirts and parkas, work boots and low heels–
for the candlelight service on Christmas Eve.
At the pastor's urging, people speak their thanks
for whatever God has given them.
One lady near the front says she is thankful
God has brought visitors to their church–
meaning me and my wife.
So I speak up and say on behalf of the visitors
that we're happy to be there and to be part of that company.
In a candlelit silence
I start thinking about the Christmas card
inscribed by a well-meaning friend:
"If you were arrested for being a Christian,
would there be enough evidence to convict you?"
The candle flame in my wife's small hand
trembles and wavers, as if not sure.
I hold my own there beneath hers
until it grows strong again,
the way I would give her anything.
As we leave, a lady hands us a brown paper bag
with an apple, orange, and tangerine,
loose nuts and candy in the bottom:
gifts of the Magi we'll feed the kids for breakfast.
We button our coats and walk out
below the blue neon cross above the door
into the crystal night of stars,
the candle breath and light of baby Jesus
still in our stricken faces.
We drive home holy, holding hands,

singing Christmas with each other,
born again, this between us,
the only evidence we need.

Third Generation Farming

The young red bull in our lower pasture
bellows across the sun-swept evening field,
frustration stamped into the dust.
He walks the fencerow constantly,
head turned north, straining the breeze
to rediscover cows across the rise.
He moves heavily, tests the fence posts
with his stubborn head. I envy him,
so sure of what he wants and needs.
For him, this is the law. If he knew
I have the power to open gates,
to free his lust upon any willing cows,
he'd bow his head when I walk by
and he'd look at me with different eyes.
I pull the tractor into the dark shed,
not tired of farming but tired
of the relentless never having enough,
and walk the tenuous beam of light
cast from the kitchen window
back to where the ends always seem to meet.
Early, through the soft breathing
of our still dark house,
I walk out to lean against the gate
where breath ghosts mill about black shapes
of cattle lowing their communal and unspeakable loss.
I go back in, find my small son in the dark
and hold his sleeping body hard against my chest
until I can almost put my hands on what it is.

Aching Hands

My best gloves won't stay on for anything,
won't keep these farmer's hands
from growing rough and cracked in the cold
or keep them from aching
in the heat of the woodstove.
I bend an hour over the bathroom sink,
scouring black dirt and grease
from knuckles and fingernails,
rubbing hand cream into my palms
and thinking of your breasts warm and sleek
beneath the red satin gown from Christmas.
At last I stand here naked in the dark
beside our bed, hands rubbed raw and clean,
listening to the lightness of your breath
as your comfortable breasts rise and fall
in sleep.
Last night I dreamed about your new boss—
the way he smiles at you, the way you talk of him,
how his hands are smooth and warm
as the light in polished cedar.

Moon with Crow

Across our farm in each of six dark ponds
swims a silver moon.
Up drinking before dawn,
I count them–six of them–
each one slightly farther from the shore.
Red spars of morning light
lean across the tops of trees,
the green depths and fields awake
to their everyday swirling dance.
A woman can be like that.
The ponds of night burst into flame
like magicians' plates of fire
where folded messages from the audience
disappear, then reappear
as white doves in the hand
that blaze up for a moment
like a love affair.
I knew a woman once
with yellow hair
like moonlight spilling.
I would have followed her
anywhere.
A single black crow races against itself
into the trees where the night must go
to cower.
A man can be like that,
nursing the dark wound in himself
in silence–
until he is right,
until there is nothing else to say.

Orchard Voices

A farmer's daughter, she had seen it all:
the flowers' careless colorings and scents
cast to and fro, the bees' insane roaring
in the apple trees,
the insolent nuzzling of the stallion
among the willing mares,
the arrogant shoving of the bull upon the cows—
purposeful matings the natural order—
the casualness of it all.
Her summer afternoons in the cool air of the river
beneath the trees with the farmhand's son
seemed just as natural. Then the marriage at 17,
the piece of land, the plowing, planting,
rain and sun, the first pregnancy
ending in the fall down cellar stairs
and dismal burial in the orchard
of an unnamed dark-eyed girl,
the black despair that everyone said would heal eventually
and so it seemed as other children came.
There was so much life around her
the shady orchard became a place for walks alone.
Two sons have gone away.
Her husband died three years ago.
She walks in fallen apple blossoms
like snow under the unkept trees
and thinks how one life is lived half-trapped in another
and she imagines a naked unnamed child glistening
in the roots, sliding through the trees, wanting out,
trying to call out through the leaves...Mother...
Sometimes she sits here with all the flowers fallen
while so green at heart
and bends to touch her face against the soft spring grass
just to feel it breathe.

Home Baking
(for mother)

"Sister and I laughed too much.
Stepmother slapped me with the tin spatula
we gave her for Christmas.
I fought the tears, went out to the barn,
climbed up cold thick rungs,
pressed my face down hard
against the gray boards of the dark loft,
felt spatula slots burn and swell and ooze
like red slugs across my cheek.
I peered through the cracks,
squinted against the brightness of the snow
and watched sister look for me in the hedge,
listened to her call from the back porch all afternoon
until the snow began to glisten pink,
until father came home tired and dark.
I would not cry, especially then.
And I knew in the warm house
sister would be snug at father's knee,
his big hard hand stroking her brown hair,
stepmother behind him in the ritual kneading
of his thick neck, a smile across his face,
the smell of baking heavy in the air."

Aftershave

Having shaved my father, adrift
in the cold rage of the nursing home,
I lay my face against his
to test the smoothness of his cheek.
For a moment I hold us together
the way he would when he'd come into my room
to say goodnight.
And the way I would have followed him,
he follows me with his eyes as I turn away.
I walk quickly down the hall
past the reaching arms of others,
frost of their uncharmed faith
stretching from their hands.
I walk past them all, aloof and inexhaustible,
my father's aftershave clinging to my face.
I walk past them all, cool as ice
that breaks loose from its own shore
and, breaking, falls away.

Susan

I am thinking about a girl from 20 years ago
named Susan
who had a boyfriend in the Air Force.
I wish I had met her for our solitary picnic
behind the girls' gym on graduation night
as I promised.
And I wonder if she went back there,
happy in the dark,
and I wonder how long she may have stood there,
nervous in her graduation gown and cap,
looking at her tin Timex watch
as the close railroad cars rumbled south
on the L&N line to Nashville,
ice melting in the cups of Pepsi, fingernails
manicured for the biggest night of her life
clutching that paper bag filled with hamburgers
and French fries from Perk's Drive-In.
Susan of wink and grin
and reach across the aisle and pinch,
who admired my bad handwriting,
who laughed at my stupid jokes,
who shared the chocolate chip cookies from Home Ec,
small blonde goddess of Miss Phipps' geography class
who loved the magic names of faraway places with me,
I'm sorry I stood you up.
Call me if you read this.
I have been to war.
I've been shot down in flames.
I've been drunk.
Susan, I've been to the places we talked about.
I have things to tell you.

Making Pearls

Because you wore his ring on a chain around your neck
and someone else wore mine,
our trips to this beach were always just as friends.
But suntan oil is an elixir of touch,
an aphrodisiac too strong for high school loyalties.
One warm night we stayed after dark
and left the top of your two-piece drifting in the surf.
You laughed about how grains of biting sand
folded within soft flesh make pearls.
We drove sixty miles past the exit to our town
before you said,
"No, we have commitments we must honor."
Today, half a lifetime and a family later,
I drive back here and catch myself
looking for the top of that leopard skin two-piece,
wanting to write you messages in the sand,
half-expecting you to show–
as if years of going back to our commitments
could be erased in a single swirling of the tide
and we might drive on into the night,
not ever looking back,
as if fingers slick with oil
could ever grasp and keep that perfect one
from a basket full of pearls.

Farmer's Market

I'm driving to town, bushels of sweet corn
in my old pickup
rusting into its own planned obsolescence
while the maladjusted lifters clatter
in the head and the worn-out clutch
grinds and grabs and whines
each time I force another gear.
Construction narrows the freeway to one lane
where the traffic thickens and binds
like our stupid cows in the barn at milking time.
So I take the exit at First Street,
stopping at the light beneath the trees
that shade the whores and winos there
in front of the old motels and bars.
I watch these honest whores—who know
everybody pays a price to love or be loved—
standing at the curb in their impartial bodies
wrapped in leather and fishnet stockings,
smoking, brushing hair, leaning in the shadows.
I catch a whiff of dark perfume
and imagine trying to talk to one of them,
how she might call me Doll or Baby
and she'd say, "You're a good-looking guy.
A guy like you shouldn't look so lonely.
Don't you need a little company?"
I'd be embarrassed and I'd say, "No.
Heck, no! I'm married. Don't I look married?"
I'd ask directions for the bridge to downtown,
I'd feel dumber than I look
and those whores would chew and pop their gum
and turn their heads to watch my old truck
tremble into gear and see the flakes of rust
pop off the tailgate as I grind it into second.

But one of them might wonder for a minute
how it would be to live with a farmer
on a place with cows and cats and white chickens,
with children and a shade tree in the yard.
Maybe we'd have a neon sign blink
slow and blue across our bed:
NO VACANCY...NO VACANCY
After the market, I drive back by.
The tender whores are gone.
All that's left is one old wino, fine and happy
with his nightly pint and a patch of warm summer grass
beneath his lonely neon landmark
I've grown accustomed to:
NO VACANCY...NO VACANCY

Lilith

She took Adam by the hand and led him to the stream
and the bed of ferns where she wrapped her golden legs
and arms around him.
She showed him how to use his lips,
his tongue, his teeth, his whole ecstatic body
in their simple act of worship.
They took each other with aggression:
as gluttons take a meal with greed,
the way a horse will drink with such pleasure
it will founder.
Then they sprawled among the ferns
like the lions beneath the trees,
who would flick their tails and yawn contentedly.
In the afternoon, Adam rose and stretched out his arms
to embrace his wonderful life.
He named a dozen animals
but soon grew bored and turned to look for her.
The animals without names sighed
and stood in line, waiting patiently at first.
But as the days went by, the ones with names
began looking down their noses at the ones without.
Fights broke out. Whole named and unnamed species
were wiped off the earth.
But God was watching. He was watching
like a cigar-smoking foreman in a factory,
like a time and motion study man.
He watched until he could not stand it anymore,
then made Adam sleep,
wiped his memory cleaner than a Disney film
and woke him up with Eve
who lay there on her back,
arms and legs out straight
as she let Adam do it to her

while she talked and talked and talked
about the crop that needed planting,
the beans that needed hoeing,
about the quiet time and prayer
they should save for Him.
Adam finished quickly,
reached up for a fig leaf
and slouched out to weed the garden,
trying to remember what made him love the ferns,
what made him sigh
as if his heart was full of sorrow.
There was something missing from his life,
he could feel it in his bones.

Publication Credit

All poems are selected from Dan Powers' book, *Mighty Good Land.*

(Some of the poems herein appear in slightly altered forms from the originals.)

LaVergne, TN USA
03 April 2011
222646LV00004B/1/P